TIPS AGAINST
CRIME

written from ***prison***

Richard O. Jones

W9-CKQ-099

Sandcastle Publishing

Tips Against Crime *Written From Prison*
A Crime Survival Guide for the '90s

Copyright © 1993 by Richard O. Jones
Book Interior and Cover Design by Renee Rolle-Whatley

This publication is designed to provide accurate and authoritative information in regard to the subject covered. It is sold with the understanding that the publisher is providing crime-fighting information and is not rendering legal, consulting or other professional advice. Therefore, neither Sandcastle Publishing nor the author accept liability for the consequences of placing into action any of the tips, methods or strategies described in Tips Against Crime Written From Prison, which action you take at your own risk. Furthermore, publisher assumes no responsibility for errors, inaccuracies, omissions or any other inconsistency herein. Any slights against people or organizations are unintentional.

Publisher's Cataloging in Publication
(Prepared by Quality Books Inc.)

Jones, Richard O., 1946-
    Tips against crime written from prison: a crime survival guide for the '90s / Richard O. Jones.
    p. cm.
    Includes Bibliographical references.
    Pre-assigned LCCN: 93-84435.
    ISBN 0-9627756-7-3

    1. Crime prevention. I. Title. 2. Home Security 3. Business Security.

HV7431.J65 1993   364.4

                  QBI93-774

Printed in the United States of America

6 5 4 3 2 1

For additional copies, use the order form at the back of the book or write to:
SANDCASTLE PUBLISHING, Customer Inquiries,
P.O. Box 3070, South Pasadena, California 91031-6070

Dedication

This book is dedicated to the struggle of a crime-free lifestyle, to the memory of all those innocent lives lost as a result of crime and to the plight of ex-convicts everywhere as they seek strength and courage to become positive and productive human beings.

Acknowledgements

Special acknowledgements go out to Barbara A. Harris and her daughters Comeletta and LaTasha, as well as to Doreen Shanks and her sons Kelvin and Prince for the gross embarrassment they may have suffered at my hands. And to my children, Yolanda, Roshelle, Jennifer, Roxanne and Darren Jones, I truly regret the traumatic experience of your early childhood brought on by my incarceration.

Contents

Preface

My first arrest came in 1956. My crime: stealing toys from Sears and Roebuck. My mother was barely eighteen years my senior and I was just ten at the time. My father, well, he was never part of the picture. In 1987, with five children and twenty-odd years of experience with criminal activities, I was arrested for major welfare fraud and sent to prison in 1988 to serve out a four-year sentence.

That's where I'm coming from. Nearly thirty years of my life have revolved around crime. I'm older, I'm wiser and I'm also a father. That last fact played the biggest part in turning me around. I guess my personal inner sense of right-and-wrong finally caught up with me. You could say I learned a lot in prison. About crime, sure, can't really avoid it. In fact, most of the scams and anti-crime tips I detail in this book came from my fellow inmates at Chino, Mule Creek and Soledad prisons in California. But I also learned about accountability.

It amazes me now what difficulty ordinary people have with defining accountability. It's all pretty clear to me. It means that every person is responsible for his or her actions and liable for their consequences. Of the many values that hold civilization together—honesty, kindness, generosity, decency—accountability may be the most important of all. Without it, there can be no respect, no trust, no law, and ultimately, no society.

Your responsibility as a citizen is to impose accountability on people who refuse, or have never learned to impose it on themselves. It's clear to me that external controls on people's behavior are far less effective than internal restraints such as guilt, shame and embarrassment.

Even I looked for social sympathy for my crime of major welfare fraud. My public defender told me that blaming alcoholism for my poor choices *may* have a favorable impact upon my sentence. Since I had a history of drunk driving arrests, a judge might be led to believe my mind had deteriorated to the point of unaccountability. However, the "I'm a victim too" performance never found an audience, not even with me.

Fortunately there are still communities (smaller towns usually) where schools maintain discipline and where parents hold up standards that proclaim: in this family, certain things are not tolerated - they simply are not done.

Yet more and more, especially in our larger cities and suburbs, these inner restraints are loosening. Your typical burglar and robber has none. He considers your property his property; he takes what he wants, including your life if you cross him.

In the 1960's when I was a teenage hoodlum, if a crime was committed, society was considered the victim. Now, in a stunning reversal, it's the criminal who is considered victimized by his underprivileged, disadvantaged upbringing, by the school that didn't teach him to read, by the church that failed to reach him with moral guidance, by the parents who didn't provide a stable home.

It's amazing to witness. Many others in equally disadvantaged circumstances choose not to engage in criminal activities. If we exempt the criminal, even partly, from accountability, we become a society of endless excuses where there's a loophole for everything.

We in America desperately need more people who believe that the person who commits a crime is the one responsible for it. *Case Closed!*

This trend toward permissiveness can't be reversed overnight. But certain things can be done in our homes, in our schools, and in our legal system to restore accountability to American life.

To the parents I say: you are the ones who plant, or fail to plant, the seeds of character in your children. Strive from the beginning to instill in your youngsters the capacity to feel shame by letting them know that, just as there are actions for which they can win praise, so there are others—lying, cheating, stealing—that are unacceptable and for which they will be punished. As parents, don't feel alone in your efforts to mold character. There are many non-profit organizations that teach accountability and reinforce it with peer pressure, such as Boy Scouts and Girl Scouts, churches, synagogues, Islamic temples, and YMCA's, to name a few.

To the teachers I say: your classroom is society in miniature. Don't excuse bad behavior. Get students to impose standards upon one another, and work to persuade the school administration to tighten up on discipline. I've heard of high schools where the first time a student is caught cheating on a test, he's warned; the second time, he may have to stay after school; the third, his parents are notified; the fourth, possibly expelled. Now what kind of moral development is that? If a kid that comes from an undisciplined home wants to goof-off all semester, what's stopping him? If he gets caught, the penalty is only a mild scolding from the teacher. So what. And if he's so unfortunate as to get busted cheating *two* more times, his parents will be notified. Ha, ha, ha.

Teachers, land your space ships. Observe what's happening all around you. Idiots are graduating from high school every year. Those are the lucky ones. At least they stumble upon a mediocre job with the grace of God. But what about the morons that cheated and were caught so many times that they were expelled or dropped out for reasons of their own. These are the 18-25 year-olds and even up to 30 year-olds that are strutting about town as gang members and drug pushers. Teachers, principles, parents, snap out of it! Does anybody know what time it *really* is?

How in the world can you expect a kid with no moral foundation or personal dignity to sprout into an honorable human being of probity and distinction? I know, I know, an adult, regardless of his background, must be held accountable for his own adult choices. True. But before this adult reaches his majority, his adult family has a moral duty to properly discipline him and to set a good example.

What about law enforcement? If I could say just one thing to the architects of that system, it would be: restore fair, swift, sure justice as one of the key buttresses of accountability. There is nothing unreasonable or uncivilized about stern justice, but you'd never know it from watching our judicial system in action today. Criminals don't fear the law, because in most cases its penalties are lenient, especially in regard to "first" and "second" offenders (just like school days).

Accountability is up to every one of us. No one can force it on us. We have to impose it on ourselves in countless little ways every day—by waiting our turn in line, not parking in no parking zones, by not lying about our absence from work or trying to wiggle out of jury duty. Small daily decisions like that, taken together, determine the moral fiber of a nation.

Good people don't have to stand by and let evil triumph. They can fight back, and they can start by applying high standards to the reflection in the mirror.

If I can do it, and do it successfully, after more nearly thirty years of crime, you can do it too. Just take it one day at a time.

—Richard O. Jones
March, 1993

Introduction

How To Get the Most Out of This Book

Anyone who has been a victim of crime will tell you at least three ways they could have avoided being victimized. That is the purpose of this book. It is designed to save you and your family from becoming unwilling crime victims simply because you are naive to the potential all around you.

While in prison, I regularly engaged in or overheard private conversations as to how easily victims and law enforcement could have stopped a crime by doing this thing or having been prepared with that device. Convicts regularly compare and share ideas involving scams and rip-offs in order to improve their criminal craft.

Although the police and law enforcement agencies in most cities do a fine job of protecting their residents, they can only do so much. I think it's every individual's responsibility to be minimally street-smart. The best weapons against crime are bars on windows, mace and, if necessary, a gun (as long as you know how to use it and care for it properly). The best defense against crime is knowledge. That's what readers of this book will gain. And armed with this information on how a criminal thinks and behaves, you will have reduced your level of fear. We all know that fear is one of our most vicious enemies. This book was written to give you back some measure of control; control over your fear and control over your life.

How To Use This Book

I have organized *Tips Against Crime Written From Prison* into crime categories: burglary, robbery, investment, credit, etc. Each chapter outlines certain scams you should be familiar with and then details tips you should take to protect yourself from individuals trying to con you. In most instances I'm relaying to you prison-yard talk, where the convict has told me in his own words how scams were run and what victims could have done to stop him. I have of course changed all the names of the convicts that agreed to be interviewed and paraphrased their statements. Due to the conditions of prison life, tape recorders are not allowed and most convicts are uneasy about someone writing down their every word. So I paraphrased and changed the names to protect the guilty. To differentiate their thoughts and ideas from mine, I've surrounded their words by quotes.

Read this book with the understanding that all the scams, con-games and crimes are real. The captures are real and the tips against these crimes are real. The difference between these tips and those forwarded by the usual sources; namely judges, law enforcement, criminologists, psychologists and the like, will become evident as you read. These tips come from men who have, for the most part, made their living ripping-off the system. The tips come from the law breakers themselves. They haven't been shared with the general public. Until now that is.

How Not To Use This Book

To those of you that have picked up this book to learn how to pull off these scams, I say forget it. I've left out all the vital operational aspects of these crimes so that you won't have a chance.

Just Do It!

If you really want to get the most out of *Tips Against Crime Written From Prison*, read the chapters that concern you the most first and then backtrack to the others. There is a tip, some piece of advice, that can be applied to your daily life in each chapter. Mark up the book if you need to. (Of course, if you borrowed this copy from the library or a friend, turn to the back of the book to find out how you can order a copy for yourself and your family). Make notes in the margins and then apply what you learn. Don't just read it and say, "Hey, that's a good idea. I should do that." And then don't do it. If you take the tips to heart, one day you will find yourself grateful that you were prepared. You never know. You might just save your own life.

Chapter 1

Burglary Scams

The FBI defines burglary as "the unlawful entry of a structure to commit a felony or theft." Burglary under this definition does not necessarily include the use of force to gain entry.

Any good burglar will tell you—there isn't a home that he can't enter. Technically speaking his assessment is absolutely accurate. There are, indeed, many barriers that can hamper a burglars' smooth and successful unlawful entry into your home. But even the most vigilant neighbors, well-trained watchdog, and sophisticated alarm systems are powerless if you're standing there with refreshments for the burglars as they load their truck.

BURGLARY SCAM #1:
Franco and the Moving Van

Franco T., a 48-year-old Italian, became a small-time burglar after a car accident forced him into early retirement. He worked as a professional construction worker, but due to recurring headaches, his employer's insurance carrier regarded his continued employment as a potential risk.

When Franco was terminated, his life savings were substantial enough to support his family of six for a few months. Before his savings were totally exhausted, Franco started a small gardening and landscaping business cater-

---

> *Any good burglar will tell you—there isn't a home that he can't enter. Technically speaking his assessment is absolutely accurate.*

ing to upper-income clients. He earned a sufficient income, but became bitter about his average lifestyle in comparison to his wealthy employers.

Franco went on to tell me how his two employees, both of which he learned were dishonest, stole from his clients whenever an opportunity presented itself. He determined that they could make up to $10,000 of extra income per month, if they all worked together burglarizing the homes he was contracted to landscape and maintain.

Here's how he ran the scam. Pay attention to this one, especially if you live in a big city and are about to move.

"I set-up each of us with fake Florida State drivers' licenses. Then I hired answering services to receive our messages for our phony moving service. We put index cards announcing our discount moving service on community bulletin boards in shopping plazas, supermarkets and public storage businesses. And I made sure to advertise only in middle- and upper-income communities."

"When we got a call to estimate a moving job, I went out and inspected the merchandise and gave the potential customer a low estimate if they had property worth stealing. When I was sure we had the job, I rented an unmarked moving truck and a private storage shed. The truck and the shed were rented with one of our fake ID's. I made sure we never used the same name twice to rent a truck or storage space."

"If the victims' property was really valuable, I arranged ahead of time to have the whole load sold to a used-furniture dealer. This included the appliances, furniture, jewelry, paintings, silverware, furs, guns, televisions, stereos, everything on the truck."

"Then, when we loaded the truck, instead of honoring our contract to deliver the goods to where they were supposed to go, we'd take them to our storage shed. In the rare event the customer was trailing us on the highway, then of course, we would do our job. I purchased all the necessary paperwork associated with moving contracts and uniforms for the men. And the most beautiful part was that we never had to use our own money to rent the truck because I always had the customer put up a cash deposit of at least $300."

"When I first started this scam, I went to the used-furniture dealer" [fence], Franco told me then, "and asked him if he knew a reliable crook that I could pay to rent public storage space and rent trucks in a phony name on a regular basis. My main requirement was that the man he recommended was not a drug-addict or alcoholic because they're notorious for being unreliable."

"A couple days later my fence introduced me to Pete. Pete and I agreed on the arrangements. Within two weeks my ID contact had provided Pete with 16 very authentic-looking fake Florida drivers' licenses. And we were in business."

The following week Pete rented a 20' x 15' storage space for a month. During that same week Franco put index cards announcing his discount rate moving services all over the shopping areas and advertisements in wealthy community newspapers. Three calls came into the answering service for the discount movers the first week. Franco returned their calls and made appointments to come by their home to give the prospective customers a free estimate.

"The standard moving rate was $37.50 per hour for two men, plus 15 cents per mile, gasoline and insurance charges. Franco's rates were $29.50 per hour for two men plus 10 cents per mile, gasoline, and fake insurance charges."

The first prospect that Franco visited was an elderly couple that was moving approximately 200 miles away to their newly purchased condominium. The couple estimated their household furnishings to be worth over $50,000. Franco collected three hundred dollars deposit, and had them pay $20 for insurance and scheduled their moving date for the following week.

At the next potential customers' home, an elegant four-bedroom, Franco estimated their personal property to exceed $150,000. This was a family of four; husband, wife and two children. This family even paid an extra $50 to have their car driven the 75 mile journey to their larger and more expensive new four-bedroom home. Franco accepted their $300 cash deposit and their moving day was one day before the date of the elderly couple, Franco's first contract.

At his third stop Franco could not accept the job because the family insisted on being moved on a day that Franco and his accomplices would be engaged in their regular duties as gardeners.

Their new recruit, Pete, was given the proper funds and reserved a large moving truck at one location, and then went to a second location and reserved a second large moving van for the following day. On the appointed date and time Pete picked up the first truck and delivered it to Franco and his men. Franco gave his men last minute instructions to be sure their victims were not following them before they brought the goods to the warehouse.

Franco told me that when his men arrived at their moving site they were greeted at the front door by an anxiously awaiting *Mr. and Mrs. Victim.* The victims had already done all their own packing and, as instructed, had labeled all their boxes. The movers had the victims sign a phony work order and, very professionally, proceeded to load the moving truck.

Occasionally Mr. Victim would assist in handling the heavier items and Mrs. Victim gave them coffee and donuts during their morning break. Within four hours of their arrival the movers had completely emptied the house and were now standing at their truck taking written instructions from Mr. Victim, although they assured him they had a map, on the best route to their (his) destination.

Mrs. Victim had already gone on ahead in their station wagon with the two children. Her husband would be driving their second car, a 1983 Jaguar, and one of the movers would be driving their 1984 Lincoln Continental. The movers were becoming concerned their first job would be spoiled because Mr. Victim was insisting that he follow them closely in traffic during the entire journey.

Apparently, the caravan trio had traveled about 1 1/2 miles in traffic, when the driver of the Jaguar exited from the car at a stop and walked back to the trailing two vehicles. He told each driver to continue on without his escort because he was returning to his old neighborhood to retrieve a borrowed blender from his ex-neighbor.

When the Jaguar was completely out of sight, the moving van, and the Lincoln Continental proceeded directly to the public storage space, 40 miles away. Four hours later the four burglars had already finished their entire operation, and were relaxing in their homes.

Franco then told me that the next morning Pete and one other accomplice drove the second rental truck to the home of the anxiously waiting elderly couple. While he met with his fence connection and negotiated a lucrative deal for yesterdays' merchandise, including the 1984 Lincoln, the two moving men were being treated to sandwiches and fruit juice at the home of the elderly couple.

After loading the moving van, the burglars informed the couple that they would be at their new condominium in 3 1/2 to 4 hours. The couple wished them a safe trip as they waited for their daughter to arrive, to drive them to the airport. They had planned to fly there and be waiting when the men arrived with all their property. Unfortunately, their property never arrived.

The Outcome

Franco and his men continued this scam for six months, operating at least once, but no more than twice per month. Franco advertised only once a month, always in different cities and always using different truck rental and public storage companies. At the end of six months Franco estimated that the total property stolen was worth over one million dollars. This burglary quartet had each accumulated substantial savings. Franco sold his landscaping service to one of his two employees and he and his family moved to California.

The moving van scam continued and no members of that team were ever arrested or brought in for questioning. Franco, however, was later arrested, convicted and sentenced to prison in California on unrelated charges.

TIPS AGAINST CRIME

Here are Franco's tips for reducing your risk of being caught with the moving van scam.

- Patronize reputable companies.

- Ask friends/acquaintances for reliable recommendations.

- If you choose to use an unknown service:

  —Ask the company representative to show identific tion.
  —Ask the company for at least two verifiable refer ences.
  —Write down the license number of the truck.
  —Ask to see registration papers on the truck.
  —Ask who their insurance carrier is and verify.
  —If any moving service fails to satisfy the above
      requests, proceed with extreme caution at your own risk.

- Keep your valuable papers and jewelry in your possession, even when dealing with a reputable company.

BURGLARY SCAM #2:
The Parking Lot Burglary Ring

Craig H., a 35 year-old Caucasian convict currently serving two to five years for burglary, says his philosophy has always been, "Why should you break into a home, when you can politely ask the home owner for and receive their front door key?"

Craig has a 37-year-old brother named David, that is also serving a two to five year prison sentence at another California prison on the same charges. Craig and David were the leaders of a burglary ring operating in Northern California during the latter end of the 1980's. The brothers had at least two dozen accomplices that were essential to their success. None of their accomplices was arrested.

Craig and David preyed on the vulnerability of minimum-wage-earning parking lot attendants and their desire to supplement their income to lure them into this scheme.

They would select elegant restaurants, hotels, country clubs, and high-rise office buildings that had valet parking for their patrons. Then they would become regular patrons of the establishments and create a good relationship with the head parking lot attendant by being friendly, tipping big, and occasionally giving the attendant a stick or two of marijuana.

When they were pretty sure they had the attendants admiration, David or Craig, (depending on which one was baiting this particular attendant), would approach him with an easy money proposition that was too good to reject. The parking lot lead employee would be told that they could earn up to $900 per week for providing duplicate keys to the cars and home of their regular parking lot customers. With these duplicate keys they must also furnish make, model and license number of the customers' car, the address on their automobile registration card and a schedule of how often and for how long this individual frequented the establishment. The attendant was told he would get $300 for each complete packet of keys and information he furnished, and that to get three complete packets per week should not be difficult. The attendant would have to risk taking the customers' keys to a nearby key cutting service and returning it before the customers returned for their automobile.

Normally, the attendant expressed reservations, (which Craig and David expected), in leaving the premises for an hour with a customers' keys. To circumvent this predicted obstacle Craig or David would suggest that this low-wage earner become an independent contractor and purchase his own portable battery-operated key cutting machine. He could use it as he sat in the automobile and it would take less than five minutes to duplicate a key. The only problem here, the attendant would be told, was that the machine cost $1,200 and was only available to state-licensed locksmiths.

However, a brand new machine could be sold to them and the cost could be deducted in exchange for the first four complete information packets with keys. To this news the attendants always rejoiced. In actuality, Craig revealed to me, he and David bought the key duplicating machine from an underground mail order business in Oregon, for $195 each.

The machines, that were about the size of a shoe box and weighed about 25 pounds, would be sent to the attendant's home by mail directly from Oregon with an enclosed invoice marked $1,200 prepaid. On delivery the receiver would have to sign for the package, and the signed receipt would be sent to the company in Oregon, they in turn forwarded it to Craig and David in California so the brothers would have proof the machine was delivered.

The package that arrived at the home of this new, independent contractor was complete with written and illustrated instructions on care, maintenance and key duplicating. Also included, was a folder containing a variety of 100 uncut key slates. The brothers never had any of their entrepreneurs attempt to defraud them. They all were excited about this opportunity their friend was giving them.

Once a week Craig or David would make their regular rounds to the parking lots where they had an insider working and collect their week's supply of wealthy patrons' house keys, car keys, home addresses and regular schedules.

After the brothers obtained this information they would drive by these homes for a brief inspection and eventually put the house under surveillance, to ascertain the number of occupants and their regular comings and goings. If the brothers were victorious in obtaining their preys' home phone numbers, this would enhance their knowledge of the residents habits by calling the house at various hours.

"It would usually take a couple of weeks of constant surveillance before we could schedule a hit," says Craig. "Sometimes the best time to burglarize a home was when it was occupied in the middle of the night. This was the case when we knew the home was always occupied, but on certain nights of the week, the parents went out and stayed late and left the children home asleep."

"We specialized in taking jewelry, guns, cash, securities, fur and silver. Therefore, we had no need of a van or truck. Our regular passenger car was always sufficient. If we discovered, after weeks of staking out a family, that burglarizing their home would be too risky, we were always comfortable in the fact that their automobile was still vulnerable to theft. Our home burglary rate was high, however. We actually hit over 70 percent of the homes we put under surveillance. And we stole about 85 percent of all the cars that we had keys for."

THE OUTCOME

"By the time my brother and I got busted in a home in Sacramento, California, we had sold 25 key-cutting machines to parking lot attendants and had burglarized over 300 homes and stolen over 800 cars. Our operation lasted for four years and when we were arrested in 1987 our conviction only included four burglary charges."

"The way we got busted was, a neighbor witnessed my brother and I entering the home of a family away on vacation. It was 3:00 a.m., and this neighbor couldn't sleep and decided to come outside and sit on the front porch. From her viewpoint across the street she saw us in their driveway and then saw us go into the house through the front door with a key. Apparently, the neighbor knew the phone number of where the family was vacationing, phoned them immediately and asked if they had given anyone permission to be entering their home at this time of the morning and with a door key."

"The vacationing neighbors thanked the nosy neighbor and asked her to call the police, and said they would immediately be returning home. When David and I exited that home at about 3:30 a.m. we found it surrounded by police."

"The big unsolved mystery for the homeowners and the law enforcement agencies was how we obtained their duplicated door keys. Our method of operation had been so similar to other recent burglaries that we felt it in our best interest to confess to at least three others. Since no one ever figured out our inside contacts, the only thing the cops could suggest to the victims was to change their door locks."

TIPS AGAINST CRIME

Here are Craig's tips to protect yourself against parking lot burglary operations

- Whenever you leave your car in the custody of a parking attendant, leave only your ignition key.

- Always remove the auto registration from the vehicle when you leave. This is more of a necessity when you are a regular customer of any parking lot. However, regular practice is still the best policy.

- Never leave spare house keys in flowerpots, mailboxes, under doormats, above door frames, in auto glove compartments, under auto seats or floor mats.

- Don't become a frequent or expected customer at any restaurant.

BURGLARY SCAM #3:
The Syndicate

There are many burglars that moonlight as legitimate sales and service people in order to have welcomed access to your home, to inventory and appraise your property. Here is how three men who called themselves "The Syndicate" did the job.

Larry E., a 28-year-old Latino prisoner serving three years for burglary, owned a small carpet cleaning service in Orange County, California. The company catered exclusively to the middle- and upper-income homes of Orange County. As a gimmick to attract more business, Larry's company would offer free window and door cleaning to customers having more than two rooms, or 200 square feet of carpet shampooed.

On the occasion that Larry had to clean the outside doors and windows of these wealthy homes, he would inwardly relish. For these were opportunities for him to search the circumference of the home for hidden door keys. The most common hiding places were door and window lintels, in and underneath flowerpots, inside fuse boxes, in mailboxes, and under doormats.

The keys would not be removed by Larry, but he would always make a notation in a memo book of the keys' location. Other notes he would inscribe in this memo book were items within the home that were portable and valuable, the location of any safes, jewelry drawers, and whether or not the home had a burglar alarm system. If so, he would note the type, make, model location of main control, and all other pertinent information.

There are many burglars that moonlight as legitimate sales and service people in order to have welcomed access to your home, to inventory and appraise your property. Be aware!

The memo book was more valuable to Larry than the good reputation his carpet cleaning service had earned in its five-year existence. The contents of this memo book were the lifeline of his lucrative burglary operation.

Larry was a member of a burglary syndicate with two close friends, Steve P., a Latino, 28-year-old electrician employed at a burglar alarm company, and Gus M., a Latino, 29- year-old locksmith and safe builder. The three men attended high school together in 1977, and remained friends through the years.

Each man operated this own independent burglary operation in Southern California, but often they collaborated on a large heist. The trio had a joint savings account that required the signature of any two of them to withdraw money. Each man faithfully deposited $100 per week into the account for the exclusive purpose of posting bail and the legal defense of the group member in need.

Although each man was married with children, they would purposefully seek out women that were in a professional position to provide itinerary information of wealthy traveling homeowners. These women would be employed in private boarding schools as teachers or counselors, travel agencies or pet hotels.

Larry told me that during one particular month, he realized that he had some exceptionally promising burglary choices. He had recorded nine hidden key locations, and six of the nine homes had no dogs or burglar alarms. Four of these six homes were occupied solely by elderly persons, and two of these were widows who lived alone. So Larry decided he would hit three of the nine targets he had marked the previous month.

He always allowed at least one full month to elapse before he burglarized a home he had marked so his victims were much less likely to think of him as a possible suspect.

The three homes were chosen on the basis of their vulnerability; no alarm system, no dog, no children, rear access, and their valuables; each home possessed an expensive personal computer and the owners lived well.

Two homes were occupied by elderly couples that belonged to several social clubs and were often away from home attending charity benefits, political dinners, and other social affairs. The third home was the residence of a middle-aged, divorced nightclub owner who was often at the club until 3:00 a.m., and didn't arrive home until about 3:30 a.m.

Larry knew from experience that the weekend would be the ideal time to successfully burglarize all three homes, and if he was extremely lucky, all on the same night. It was on Friday night about 8:30 p.m. when Larry dialed the phone number of one of the elderly couples' homes. The phone had rung seven times, and just as Larry had decided they weren't at home, the receiver was picked up and a man said: "For Christ's' sake, Douglas, we're on our way! Helen is waiting for me in the car this moment. I have the tickets in the palms of my hands....Goodbye!" And with that he slammed the receiver into its cradle.

Larry called the remaining two phone numbers; one couple was at home, but the other, the nightclub owner, was out and had left instructions on an answering machine as to where he could be reached.

At eleven o'clock Larry left his elegant four-bedroom home in Diamond Bar, California, en route to his first engagement in Anaheim Hills, a city in Orange county, roughly a 20-minute freeway drive. When he arrived in the neighborhood of the couple that were out for the evening, the time was approximately 11:30 p.m. Larry went to a nearby public telephone and called their number again. This time the phone range ten times before Larry hung up.

He walked back to his five-year-old Chevrolet station wagon that he only drove on his burglary missions. Larry circled the block twice being especially alert to his environment; trees, cars, windows, any movement. He needed to act quickly. He drove his car into the alley behind the home and jumped the fence. He moved hastily to the rear porch and removed a key from a hanging flowerpot a couple of inches above his head. With key in hand, he proceeded around the side of the house to the front door. On the front porch he slipped on his ski mask and gloves. Without knocking or ringing the bell as a final precaution, he entered the home with the front door key. His first stop was in the bedroom, where he searched for and found lots of jewelry, some cash, two rifles and one hand gun. He put all this in the huge dark-green plastic trash bag he carried.

He disconnected the portable color TV and VCR in the bedroom and carried all this valuable loot through the kitchen onto the back porch. Once in the back yard Larry rushed to the rear gate, unlocked it and carried the goods to his station wagon. The time now was 12:15 a.m. After putting his loot in his car he hurried back to the house for a second search. This time he unloaded into his car a microwave oven, another portable color TV, more jewelry and two typewriters. The time was now 12:35 a.m. He rushed back a third time for the grand prize, the expensive IBM personal computer.

In all his haste, Larry hadn't noticed the 1988 Fleetwood Cadillac with two couples inside, parked in the driveway and hidden from view by the fence separating the back yard from the front yard.

The homeowners, arriving home with house guests, later testified in court: "I noticed something was wrong the moment we were within a couple of houses from our house", said Mr. Wilcox, (not his real name), "because our driveway gate was not shut tight as I knew it was before we left home." Mr. Wilcox testified that he then doused his headlights before turning into the driveway.   Mr. Wilcox was a 64-year-old, retired sergeant of the California Highway Patrol and his son was employed as a Los Angeles police detective. They had been out that evening celebrating Doug and his wife Linda's seventh wedding anniversary. The couples had planned to spend the night together after a late dinner and show, and then go boating early Saturday morning.

The elder Mr. Wilcox testified that when he stepped onto his front porch he observed a trail of dirty footprints leading to his front door, but there were no footprints leading away from the door.

The young Mr. Wilcox observed the same conditions and immediately signaled his father to wait 30-seconds before entering, he was going to the rear door and they would enter simultaneously. Both men looked briefly at their wrist watches, and off Doug Wilcox went down the driveway with his revolver in his hand.

Detective Doug Wilcox testified that when he reached the backyard he could see the rear gate leading to the alley was ajar. And as he approached the rear porch, although the kitchen and porch light were out, it was clear that a suspect was inside the home. The back door stood wide open and the sound of footsteps could be heard running across the hardwood floor in the hall. He continued to say that he'd waited until the 30-second point before entering the rear in combat position. Approximately five seconds later he heard his father yell, "Freeze you son-of-a-bitch!" then the sound of a loud crash which he guessed was his mother's computer."

Larry E. later revealed as he told this story to me while walking the yard of the California State Prison in Soledad, in February of 1990, that as the old man was handcuffing him he remarked to his son, "I would've shot this son-of-a-bitch if I hadn't recently paid some cleaning service to clean our carpets. Bloodstains all over the place, who needs it?" Then his son removed my ski mask and the old man gasped, "I'll be damned! This is the asshole that cleaned our fuckin' carpet!" Larry and I got a good laugh.

When Larry E. got booked into the police station, his first phone call was to his buddy, Gus M. and together they located a bail bondsman. Larry's bail was $25,000. By 4:00 a.m. that Saturday morning, only three hours after his arrest, he walked out of the police station to the salutes of his syndicate.

The consensus among the trio was that the wisest move Larry could make was to remain on bail as long as possible, taking advantage of every legal extension and loophole to buy more time. "Prison would definitely be part of my future, the only true negotiating I would be involved in would be bargaining for a reduced sentence. The decision was made not to spend sumptuously on a futile cause, but instead limit our attorney fees to $10,000 and take the best deal we could get."

Since Larry had been convicted of burglary in the past, and his current charges were connected to a well-planned scam, Larry and his buddies knew his chances of receiving a light sentence were between comatose and dead. The syndicate agreed they would work on a big job per month in which Larry would receive 40% of the profit and the 60% would be split equally between the other two. Each man agreed to tap their sources, the gullible women they kept in reserve, for more lucrative burglary jobs.

As the weeks went by Larry began to increase his own independent burglary operation. The first job he pulled after his arrest was the middle-aged divorced nightclub owner named Bill. The job turned into a personal vendetta to compensate for his arrest. First he called Bill's home to get an idea of Bill's whereabouts. He got the usual recording and decided 10:00 p.m. would be a good time to strike. At 10 p.m. Larry circled Bill's block for a visual inspection. After his personal safety concerns were satisfied, he drove through the alley in his recently purchased 8 year-old van. (His station wagon was impounded as evidence.)

He parked at the back gate, exited the van and reached over the gate and unlocked it. Once in the yard he retrieved Bill's house key from beneath a rock near his kitchen window. Larry crept to the front and inserted the key: the door opened easily. The first item he took to his van was Bill's personal computer.

On the next trip he quickly discovered a safe in the rear of a hall closet. It sat on the floor and was about four feet high, two feet in length and one-and-a-half feet in width. To open it required by-passing two locks. A combination lock on the door, and a key lock on the side of the door.

"My heart began to race," Larry explained, "as I thought about the situation." Rather than waste time trying to open it, Larry decided to take it. He went back to his van and got his hand-truck. This hand-truck was built to handle up to 1500 pounds, and Larry estimated this safe to be about 1000 pounds.

After he strapped the safe to his hand-truck, he was able to maneuver this 1/2 ton chuck of steel up a slippery hill. By the time he finished huffing and puffing, two hours had passed and he was finally closing the back door to his van with his 1/2 ton crackerjack box.

When Larry finally got home it was 2:00 a.m. He locked the van in the garage and retired for a few hours sleep, for at daybreak he had six customers expecting their carpets cleaned. Larry had called his burglary buddies to meet him at his house that evening and asked Gus to bring his tools. When the men arrived it was approximately 7:45 p.m. They adjourned to the garage and proceeded to work on busting this iron piggy bank.

Gus used blowtorches, crowbars, sledgehammers, files, drills, and hack saws in his three-hour assault on the safe. "Steve and I," Larry states, "relieved Gus every so often and followed his instructions as he looked on." Finally at 11:00 p.m. Gus got the three-hundred pound door open.

The safe contained three shelves about ten inches apart on the top portion of the safe. Each shelf was fully packed with stacks of money. The top shelf held fives, tens and twenties; the second shelf was the home of fifties and the third shelf was the home of photographs of Benjamin Franklin, one hundred dollar bills. The total sum was over $300,000.

The bottom portion of the safe contained 30 kilos of cocaine with an estimated value of over $400,000. It was obvious that Bill, the nightclub owner, was also a heavy dealer in drugs. That night we loaded the safe back into my van and drove to the beach about 40 miles away and dumped the safe on shore.

Larry says he continued to work , occasionally doing an easy, independent burglary. A couple weeks later Steve called a meeting at his home. During the meeting Steve informed his cohorts that he had reliable information, from an admiring female insurance underwriter, that a certain millionaire's home in Beverly Hills would be vacant for three days.

The home would have over $1,600.000 in jewelry in the safe. Steve said the home was wired with a modern burglary alarm system. One which he was thoroughly familiar with and could disable in a matter of seconds. Steve went on to describe the model and make of the wall safe on the property and Gus assured us that he could open the safe within 15 minutes.

Steve said that the home would be free of all servants and caretakers for the three-day period. On the following Thursday night these homeowners would leave and not return until Sunday night. Steve told Gus and Larry that he bought two large sheets of black magnetic plastic that could be cut into business size signs and applied to the sides and rear of Larry's unmarked burglar-mobile, and they could paint the name of the fictitious landscaping company on the signs. This would give them the appearance of a legitimate landscaping service with the authority to be on the premises.

The plan was to use Larry's lawn care equipment for this daylight burglary. Larry and Steve would remain outside the house, cutting grass, trimming bushes, watering, raking, etc., while Gus worked on the safe inside.

It was mutually agreed that Saturday would be the perfect day for the heist since the syndicate was off their regular jobs on this day. They met at 7.00 a.m. at Larry's home, on the morning of the planned burglary. They drank coffee and talked of their mischievous school days as they loaded the van with lawn service equipment and meticulously attached the freshly painted lawn service signs to the vehicle. Steve supplied each man with dark green jumpsuits with their phony business name on the back and their fake first names on the left breast pocket.

"When we arrived at the home in Beverly Hills," said Larry, "I discovered it was a huge mansion sitting on six or seven acres. I drove the van into the circular driveway and all the way around, past the front entrance, to the far side of the mansion and backed up to the rear yard entrance gate. We unloaded the equipment in a couple of minutes. It was previously decided that we would work around the outside for 45 minutes before any attempt to disarm the alarm system. This would ease the minds of any suspicious neighbors and arouse any sleeping occupant that may be inside. Also, this allowed plenty of time for any police arrivals if anyone or any electrical system alerted them. At this point we could easily explain that we're just three lost Mexican gardeners at the wrong house."

After circling the property several times Steve was positive about the alarm system. He even discovered that we were being videotaped by two surveillance cameras that we had activated upon entering the property. With both cameras operating the entire perimeter of the mansion was being recorded. Also, Steve discovered that anyone weighing more than approximately 20 pounds would trigger a third camera if they came within six feet of the front door. There also was an audio and silent alarm that would go off if anyone tampered with any door or windows or entered the patio areas.

When Larry and Gus heard this depressing news, they both looked at Steve with a questioning expression. Steve gave them a reassuring grin that spoke for itself, saying "No problem." Then Steve said, "You guys remove those cameras from each of those trees. And don't worry about setting off any alarm, the cameras aren't connected to the alarm system. I'll remove the third camera hidden above the front door entrance." We went our separate ways to fulfill our assignments. Gus and I used the ladders we had to reach the cameras. Steve stood on a yard chair to remove his assigned camera.

"When I stepped one foot onto the first step of my ladder", Larry explained, "I noticed that attached to the tree was a five-by five-inch piece of veneer that was painted to blend in with the tree bark. The veneer was impaled with a single brown nail at the top. With slight fingertip pressure to the right or left side of the veneer, the shield swayed.

There was a small, natural aperture in the tree and inside this space, a zip type sandwich bag. "I reached in and withdrew the bag," said Larry, "and Eureka!" I quickly removed the video camera and went to share our good fortune with my partners. By the time I reached the front of the house where Gus and Steve had been stationed, Steve had already removed his camera and was around the side working on disconnecting the alarm system. Gus had also retrieved his camera and was putting it in the van. I joined him there. I put my camera in the trash box with the other two cameras and covered them with grass and leaves. Then I showed Gus my findings. Extra house keys. Three keys on a small ring. We both figured the smallest key turned the alarm and the two regular size door keys were for the front door.

We both walked at a swift pace to inform Steve. When we reached Steve he was lying on his back with half his body through a small transom at the base of the building. He apparently saw my feet near his hips and shouted, "Anything wrong?"

"No," Larry replied, "I found some keys and I'm sure they'll open the front door." "Good," answered Steve, "I'm finished here, the outdoor alarm is inert." Steve then slid out of the transom. He looked at the keys and smiled, then confessed his concern that although there was no longer an outside alarm, we might have tripped an inside alarm upon entering through any ground floor door or window. Therefore, he planned for Gus to enter through the second floor window, because if there was an interior alarm it would most likely be monitoring the first floor.

"The upstairs rooms are free of alarms and the safe is upstairs in the master bedroom. But with these keys, Gus can enter through the front door and turn off the interior alarm." "Yeah," Gus added, "the control box is probably within a few feet of the front door. I'll have to turn it off immediately."

Gus went through the front door after using both keys and quickly closed the door behind him. Steve and Larry continued to do yard work. He looked at his watch, Larry told me, and the time was 10:10 a.m. They had been at the mansion for 70 minutes. Three minutes later, at 10:13 exactly, a middle-aged female came jogging up the driveway to the front door. She smiled at Steve and cheerfully greeted him. Then she noticed Larry on the far side of the yard and waved warmly in his direction. The woman then turned to Steve who stood about 200 feet away raking through the flower bed and said, "Don't mind me, I come by daily to feed the cat while the Brunners, (not their actual name), are away." They noticed a set of keys that were in her hand and she disappeared through the front door, closing it behind her.

Steve and Larry exchanged glances and continued their work. Meanwhile, Gus was upstairs decoding the combination lock on the safe. Gus said to his buddies later, "Just as I heard the first tumbler drop, I almost panicked when I heard a woman's voice saying, *Here kitty, kitty*. Then I heard this cat meow. And after a minute of complete silence, the phone rang. The woman answered on the second ring, "Brunner's residence, this is Mrs. Jacobsen, (not her actual name), speaking." Then she sounded contrite as she explained, "But Sergeant, I'm sure I did turn it off." There was a pause..."Okay, sorry for the trouble, I'll turn it off now." Then the woman went to the alarm box near the front door and inserted a small key and turned it.

When Gus entered the home he turned the alarm off within the 20-second time limit. When Mrs. Jacobsen entered she didn't notice that the alarm was off and turned the alarm back on, alerting the security guard station that someone was in the home.

Security companies generally phone clients' homes to make sure the homeowner hasn't accidentally tripped the alarm. If no one answers the phone, or if an unauthorized person answers, or the security company suspects foul play for any reason, the dispatcher will send armed guards to investigate. Apparently Mrs. Jacobsen was familiar to the security company and they found no reason to investigate further. Now when the good neighbor left the home she would turn the alarm on again which meant anybody walking on the first floor would trip the signal.

After Mrs. Jacobsen had fed the cat and brought in the mail, she went to the front door and turned the alarm back on before leaving the mansion. Gus walked as fast as he could back to the control switch and turned the alarm power box off. Then he returned to the safe and resumed his mission.

At 11:15 a.m. Gus exited the front door carrying a quarter-full brown plastic trash bag. He walked casually to a van and climbed through its back door and shut the door behind him. Larry and Steve quickly loaded the equipment and entered the car. Larry drove out of the driveway, turned right and proceeded triumphantly down the street at about 20 miles-per-hour.

After driving about 1000 yards the street came to a dead-end. Larry had to make a U-turn and go back the way they came. Now as they drove past the beautiful 24-room mansion for the final time, all three men were astonished and tremendously anxious as they passed the circular driveway and saw it occupied by two private security patrol cars and the security guards walking around each side of the mansion.

The syndicate talked, laughed and rejoiced all the way back to Diamond Bar. They never opened the plastic bag until they were safely back in Larry's garage, mainly because Gus had buried it so thoroughly among the grass, weeds and leaves that the men figured they better leave it hidden, especially after seeing the investigating security guards.

The plastic bag contained even more jewelry than Steve had expected, plus $47,000 cash. The men split the money, with Larry getting $17,000 and Steve and Gus each receiving $15,000. Steve revealed to Larry and Gus, his multimillionaire employer was his "fence" and he bought anything of great value, especially jewelry and art. He would sell all this merchandise to him and they would split the return in four days.

During the four-day wait Steve told his buddies that his female accomplice had informed him that the loot was valued at two million. Steve's employer paid him a fair price for the jewelry, precious coins and rare stamp collection.

THE OUTCOME

The next few weeks went quickly and Larry had already been to court a couple of times. His next appearance was scheduled for a Monday morning and Larry planned on pleading guilty and accepting a three-year sentence. His attorney had advised him to accept the three years—if he didn't he would be facing eight.

Larry pled guilty and was scheduled for sentencing a month later. During that month Larry and his wife separated and Larry moved in with a travel agent he had been dating and getting burglary information from for two years. Larry says he holds his wife responsible for his arrest due to the fact she had not told him about the broken tail light that cost him valuable time in completing his first burglary of that night. Larry plans to terminate his burglary career with his syndicate and he and his travel agent fiancé will open their own travel agency.

TIPS AGAINST CRIME

Here are Larry E.'s tips to reduce your risk of home burglary.

- "The one thing that always stands out in my memory about how people can reduce their risk of being burglarized is to install burglar alarms. When my attorney asked Mr. Wilcox, the retired highway patrolman, why he didn't have an alarm system protecting his property, his answer was, I never thought it could happen to me." This was a man who worked in law enforcement for 30 years before retiring. Mr. Wilcox probably investigated over 500 burglaries according to his own estimate, and he left his own family vulnerable.

- If you live in a neighborhood that is predominately homeowners, and you strongly feel that you can trust your neighbor, the two of you should exchange door keys. Perhaps even a third neighbor should be involved in a three-way key exchange. That way, you can always go to one another for the key in case of emergency.

- If you prefer to hide an extra key around the outside of your home, never let anybody but the household residents know the location. If you have a gardener or housekeeper, hide your key in a place that they will never accidentally discover it. It would be best to have several outdoor hiding places and rotate your key weekly.

- Neighborhood watch programs are a very effective deterrent to professional burglars. However, most burglars are not professionals. These roguish scavengers burglarize at random, not knowing or caring about neighborhood watch programs or the contents of your home. Although neighborhood watch programs won't deter this type of criminal, they can be instrumental to their apprehension. Contact your local police department and inquire about organizing or joining a neighborhood watch program.

- An extremely effective and [esoteric] anti-burglary technique that most burglars will admit has deterred them from hitting a home, is a television being left on. Some conscientious individuals leave at least one television set on all night, every night, instead of a non-deterrent night-light.

"When a burglar sees a TV light flickering through the window of an otherwise dark home, they assume the resident is home and suffers from insomnia. Have the volume at a level that cannot be heard except in the room it's located in. The burglar will also hear these soft voices out-

---

If you prefer to hide an extra key around the outside of your home, never let anybody but the household residents know the location.

side your door or window if they prowl long enough to investigate."

"In the event the TV station is not an all-night channel, although you should select an all night channel whenever possible, and the station has gone off the air, this will further confuse the burglars because now they'll believe you will be getting up at any moment to turn the TV off. In either case, a burglar would prefer a target with fewer ambiguities."

• "I have personally known homeowners in areas with a crime rate so high that it was commonplace for at least one house or apartment on each block to be burglarized every night. However, the residents that took the extra precaution of leaving the television on, even when out of town, had far fewer break-ins than their neighbors. The extra cost in electricity is only pennies compared to the harm and loss a burglar could bring."

Chapter 2

Robbery Scams

The FBI defines robbery as "the taking or attempting to take anything of value from the care, custody, or control of a person or persons by force or threat of force or violence, and/or putting the victim in fear." It is a particularly disabilitating crime because of the fear engendered by the threat of violence. Robbery is the only one of the seven traditional FBI Index Crimes—murder, forcible rape, robbery, aggravated assault, burglary, larceny-theft—that is both a property crime and a crime of violence. As one of the class of property crimes, its prime motivation is money. There is also the likelihood that the perpetrators do not know their victims. As one of the class of violent crimes, there is a relatively high probability of victim injury and even death.

So what are the most common robbery scams? While at Mule Creek State Prison, Ione, California doing time for welfare fraud, I had a chance to talk with two big-time professional robbers: Roy and Issac. A professional thief, just like any other expert in a particular field, has a certain level of arrogance about himself. He knows when a job has been pulled by a novice and which job has the touch of a real expert. They talked with me at length about various successful scams they have pulled and then gave me some tips on how their victims could have avoided being robbed, and in one case, knifed.

ROBBERY SCAM #1:
Robber Roy Hooks Up With Hookers

Roy, a 53-year-old African-American man, convicted of 2nd degree murder/robbery now serving 21 years to life, has been to prison once before. Roy confesses that he has been a professional robber since the age of ten. "A good jackman, (robber), is hardly ever without money—never for a long period of time. I started out jacking-up elementary school kids for their lunch money when I was in the third grade. I had an average of five boys at my school that paid me five cents per day. If they didn't voluntarily pay the five cents, I would beat them up and take all they had; so they were usually willing to pay."

Roy told me that as he got older and needed more money, his small group of daily debtors got bigger, along with their payments to him. By the time he entered high school he had started an extortion ring of three and collected $5.00 per day from dozens of boys. Occasionally, if someone tried to protest, he would have them beaten up by his two assistants, or take care of them personally. In a fascinating display of thieves honor, Roy says, "Of course if we lost the fight, which rarely happened, that particular winner would never be subject to our extortion attempts again."

"When we wasn't strong-arming kids at school for money, my trio would apply our trade by jacking paperboys and snatching purses. At age sixteen I was permanently suspended from the high school I attended in Los Angeles. It was the policy of my high school that your third suspension was final. Fighting was the given cause for the suspension on all three occasions, but the real reason for the fights was robbery. I decided not to register at another school, but, instead, become a full-time robber."

Roy goes on to say that by the age of nineteen, he stood 6'5" and weighed 230 pounds. He used his size to intimidate his victims and to buy liquor and get into bars. "As a matter of fact, bars, especially bars catering to military personnel, are where I selected my robbery victims."

"In San Diego, California, the sailors were my favorite targets. There's a naval base in San Diego and on weekends the downtown bars were flooded with drunken sailors. My method for selecting victims was simple. One, he was flashing money, and two, he was intoxicated. If they met these two requirements, I would follow them on foot until the most opportune moment and then attack them, usually from the rear, with a couple hard blows with my fist to the head. Ninety percent of the time I would knock them out with one or two punches. But not always."

"During one particular struggle, this sailor and I fought seems like 15 minutes non-stop. I finally released the sailor's wrist and reached into my boot and withdrew a 10-inch hunting knife. As I stuck my knife into his side, I got some surprise help from a hooker who had followed me following my sailor. She came down on his head with an iron pipe. Blood from the sailor's head gushed down into my face as he tumbled over. My knife was still in his side when I pushed him completely off me. My rescuer was Lilly, a 20-year-old redheaded, black prostitute who hustled the local bars and rolled her customers. I had known Lilly a couple of years and on several occasions she would signal me which drunk in the bar had lots of money on him. I would follow our mark and after I had beaten and robbed him I would return to the bar and split my take with Lilly. Lilly had a superior instinct for spotting which men had a lot of money on them and also where the money was located."

"Quickly, and without passing words, we searched this unconscious sailor. I searched everywhere from the waist up and Lilly searched everywhere from the waist down. I found three hundred dollars bills in his top short pocket, and she confiscated his money belt and wallet which later turned out a total of $2800. We ran from the alley and got into the car Lilly had left parked and running at the curb. Later I learned Lilly had been following me and this drunken sailor because her 'hooker instincts' told her that he might be a problem, and she thought I might need a getaway car."

Roy went on to tell me that he and Lilly left town and went to Dallas, where they married a year later. Lilly worked as a waitress in an elegant downtown hotel where rich businessmen would routinely offer her money for sex. That's when Rob got involved and they plotted a new scam. Lilly would agree to sneak to the men's hotel room after work and accept their proposition. She would call Roy with the man's name and room number. Then after she had been in his room a few minutes, Roy would appear at the door. Lilly would be in there half-dressed or totally nude, depending on how long it took for Roy to arrive.

"If the mark didn't answer the door fast I'd knock harder. Then I would beat on the door and call out her name. She would pretend to be nervous and frightened, saying something like, *'It's my husband, he must have followed us to this room.'* Then she would say something like, *'We'd better open the door before he kicks it in, cause he's a wild man when he's angry.'* "

"Once my wife, or our mark opened the door, I'd bust in, pretending to be mad, pull my gun and threaten to kill them both. Without fail the mark would plead for his life. Lilly would be crying and begging also. Finally the man would begin bargaining for his life. Offering me all his cash and jewelry if I'd just take the woman and leave. I would first pretend to be even more angry over the offer of money. That's when my wife would interrupt with statements like, 'Roy, Roy, honey, please take the money, Mr. so-and-so here isn't trying to insult you, he only wants to help,' adding, 'Isn't that right, Mr. so-and-so?' It worked like magic. We usually collected anything from a few hundred to several thousand per hit. When Lilly returned to work the next day her mark had usually checked out of the hotel."

"We operated that robbery scam at the same hotel successfully for three years. The money was good and I had even solicited two other beautiful waitresses from two other Dallas hotels. Our joint venture was profitable to each of us."

THE OUTCOME

Rob was eventually convicted for robbery and assault and was sentenced to 17 years.

ROBBERY SCAM #2:
Robber Roy Drives Taxis

After serving 17 years, Rob was paroled and immediately relocated to California in 1982. The first job he found was as a cab driver in Los Angeles. He picked a route that would bring in good money. He worked Los Angeles International Airport and quickly discovered that he could taxi a passenger unfamiliar with Los Angeles, for double and sometimes triple the fair.

"The best way to avoid fare padding is for the customer to call the cab company before flagging a cab, and tell them your location and destination. Ask the dispatcher to tell

> *The best way to avoid fare padding is for the customer to call the cab company before flagging a cab, and tell them your location and destination.*

you the mileage and estimated fare. After you are seated in the cab, give the driver your destination and when the cab is in motion, tell the driver that the dispatcher informed you that this trip is blank miles, and the estimated cost is blank dollars. Does the driver consider that a reasonable estimate?"

"As a cab driver, the main source of my income came from jacking my drunk passengers. Anytime I had a passenger that was so intoxicated that they required my assistance in helping them in or out of the cab or up or down the stairs, I would usually pick their pockets."

"Six months of driving the cab brought me into contact with lots of hookers that were regular taxi customers, commuting from hotel to hotel all night long. It wasn't long before I was hustling customers for the girls. When a businessman entered my cab from the airport, if he was alone, I would inquire if he would like the company of a beautiful woman tonight. I told him that I knew the most sexy ladies, of all races, in town. I even had a photo album of six enticing prostitutes, in various stages of undress, including nudes. I carried a beeper and gave them my beeper number in case they were interested."

"When they settled into their hotel, they could call my service and leave their name and number. My beeper service would immediately page me. When I received their message I would return the call. We would briefly discuss which girl was available and the approximate time of arrival. The average price was $400, and twice as much if it was an overnight date. I would pick up his date from the hotel cocktail lounge or their apartment, wherever they were at the time. This arrangement worked perfectly for over 18 months. I was earning in excess of $1,500 per week, not including my taxi driver wages, tips and thefts. Most of my money was spent on cocaine."

"One rainy night, an Asian male passenger, arriving from Japan, hailed my cab at the airport. The man was travelling alone, about 60-years-old, apparently wealthy, very expensive luggage, jewelry and clothing, and intoxicated. On the trip to my passenger's hotel, I aroused his interest in a woman for the evening."

"From my photo album, he chose Nikki, a young Asian woman. I gave him my number and asked him to call me in an hour and I would let him know if his choice was available. A couple of hours passed before my beeper service signaled me. When I called them, I received a message that Mr. Wong had called. I called Mr. Wong and told him that his date was indeed interested and available, and I would deliver her within the hour. When we arrived at his hotel room, Mr. Wong answered the door clad only in undershorts. After introducing the two I whispered to Nikki to discourage the client from continued drinking, because as every hustler and hooker knows, a drunk can create a real problem. Then I gave Nikki the signal to excuse herself to the bathroom, to provide Mr. Wong and I privacy to talk."

"This is always done so the customer and I can discuss the amount of time they want and I could collect the money. I never allowed the customer to pay the girl directly nor was she allowed to be present in the money exchange. It was for her own protection, because if she didn't receive or discuss any money with the client, she can easily beat a prostitution charge."

"Mr. Wong paid me $400 and I told him that I would be back in two hours to pick up his date. Then I knocked on the bathroom door and Nikki came out. I told her that I was leaving her with my friend Mr. Wong, and would return to join the party in two hours."

This particular taxi-hooker scam didn't work out well for Rob. Upon returning to the hotel, the customer wanted a refund and threatened to phone the police because the *girl* he had hired couldn't perform to his satisfaction. They fought and Rob knocked away the lamp coming at his head then pushed the customer backwards. The man stumbled a couple of feet and fell, hitting his head hard against the dresser. Nikki, an ex-nurse, checked his pulse and pronounced him dead. Rob found $83,000 in cash in a briefcase as well as a smaller case filled with unmounted diamonds. They divided the take; Nikki $43,000 and no diamonds and the rest for Rob before wiping all fingerprints from the room and leaving unnoticed. That night Nikki and Rob parted company.

THE OUTCOME

Rob was connected to the murder via the telephone messages he'd picked up from Mr. Wong. He was eventually picked up in a San Francisco drug house raid and booked for possession of cocaine. Within a few hours thereafter, he was also informed that there was a no-bail warrant out for his arrest in Los Angeles on murder and robbery charges.

"Eventually, I pleaded guilty to second degree murder and robbery, as part of a plea bargain, to avoid life in prison without the possibility of parole. I was sentenced to 21 years to life in state prison."

TIPS AGAINST CRIME

Here are Roy's tips to reduce your risk of robbery.

"Most robbers are specialists. They specialize in a certain type of victim. Some of us prefer to hit large businesses: banks, supermarkets, new car dealerships, etc. This is because the take is usually large and the risk of deadly resistance is relatively small. I was always turned off by this type of robbery because of the great probability of witnesses, armed guards, silent alarms and electronic surveillance equipment."

"Some robbers specialize in small businesses such as gas stations, small stores and bars. This is because they're frightened by a true challenge. They are petty thieves and usually wait until they're desperate for cash before they attempt a hit. The robbery is very seldom well-planned and the robber is usually a drug user. They're insecure and don't feel they possess the skill to hit a bigger target. Usually they're intelligent, violent, angry and lethal. Fear of being caught will prompt them to kill all witnesses, even if their victims were fully co-operative."

Among the most effective deterrents against the petty thief type of robbers are:

- Conspicuously placed signs with warnings such as: private police patrol or surveillance camera on premises.

- A citizen five-band radio tuned in on police calls. Police radio calls will be continuously coming through. Have this radio placed out of the view of your customers, but be sure the broadcast can be clearly heard in the cash register areas. Don't have the police calls heard throughout the entire store. To be effective, it must appear that the broadcasts are for your ears only.

- Whenever possible, do not work in a store alone. Work with a companion or co-worker. Always try to position yourselves in the store so that it is

---

Whenever possible, do not work in a store alone.

difficult for one person to keep both of you in full view at the same time. This puts the intended perpetrators in an insecure position. This type of robber usually won't attempt a hit unless they're sure they're in full control and have the victim at an extreme disadvantage.

Rob's specialty in robbery was not businesses, but male individuals. Here's what he had to say about men and money and egos. If you recognize yourself, take note. You may be a victim sooner than you think.

"I feel that anyone carrying a large amount of cash, $500 plus is inviting trouble. Especially when that person goes to a public place and exposes to nearby onlookers much more cash than necessary to conduct his business. These men are typically either naive or fools because they want everyone to know that they have money. They foolishly think that they can't be robbed because of a false sense of machismo. Foolish women in the company of these foolish men are impressed, and this encourages more flashing. Unfortunately she doesn't realize that her companion is not only putting his safety in jeopardy, but her own as well."

- When carrying large sums of money, separate it. Estimate how much cash you will actually need over the next few hours, add a few more dollars to that amount and separate it from the cash that you'll not be in immediate need of. This surplus cash should be tucked away in your undergarments, shoes, socks or well-hidden in your automobile. Never leave it in your purse or wallet or simply put the extra money in your other pocket. This is like carrying your extra

> *When carrying large sums of money, separate it. The surplus cash should be tucked away. Never leave it in your other pocket.*

house key on the same ring. Flashing your money is not only poor judgement, but makes you look foolish.

- Going out alone, to public places, invites a robbery attempt. This doesn't apply to public places of necessity like laundromat, stores and restaurants, but to nightclubs, concerts, plays, sporting events, dances, parties and charity events. If you are under the influence of alcohol or drugs, your risk for robbery doubles.

- When you enter any social function alone, several things are assumed by the would-be robber. First, you're out to have a good time, which usually means you're receptive to friendly conversation. Second, you definitely didn't leave without enough money to afford yourself a good time, plus extra money, in case the night gets expensive.

- If you are out for the evening alone, do not leave your food and drink unattended. It's very easy to slip drugs into drinks or sprinkle them on foods.

- When customers of prostitutes go to pre-paid hotel or motel rooms, they become the favorite target of many set-up artists. If you employ the services of a prostitute, never take him/her to your home and always choose your own hotel or motel. If anyone knocks at your door, unless you've ordered room service, call down to the front desk and ask them to investigate saying you would like not to be further disturbed.
If the prostitute tries to prevent you from calling the front desk, this should alert you that you're

---

If you are out for the evening alone, do not leave your food and drink unattended. It's very easy to slip drugs into drinks or sprinkle them on foods.

about to be robbed. If the voice on the other side of door sounds threatening don't open the door, instead, hurry to the television and snatch the cable wires off. Most hotel and motels have audible or silent alarms built into the television's electrical system so that the front desk will be alerted to an attempted theft. This will initiate an investigation of your room. If you can't get to the TV or phone fast enough, throw an object through the window. This will also initiate an investigation, and, perhaps save your life.

ROBBERY SCAM #3
Armed Robbery at the ATM

Among the experienced robbers willing to share their criminal adventures with me was Issac O., a 34-year-old Caucasian sentenced to 10 years for armed robbery. A heroin addict since the age of sixteen, Issac was sentenced to prison twice by the time he was 28 years old. The first term was 18 months for possession of drugs, and the second, a four-year sentence for possession and sale of drugs. Twice he committed himself to drug rehabilitation programs in his home state of New York. The private treatment programs were costly, but his parents were wealthy and paid the bills.

He says that within three days of his last prison release he was back shooting heroin. "A few months of regular drugs had deteriorated my appearance so much," says Issac, "that the family dog wouldn't even let me walk him. I had just enough pride to be ashamed of myself, but not enough to stay clean. So rather than to continually embarrass my family, not to mention the dog, I took my Dad's car and several of his credit cards and headed for California. I called home, collect from California two weeks later. My Mom told me Dad had bought a new car, cancelled the credit cards I had in my possession, and that he never intended to speak to me again. I tried to explain that what I was doing was for their own good more than for mine. I felt it would be impossible for me to ever stay clean in New York. I explained that when I was drug-free for one full year, I would return home and make it up to her and Dad."

"My dad picked up the extension phone and yelled at me for stealing his car. He told me to keep the car and cherish it because it was the last thing I would ever get from him. And he added, *you'll never be anything but a liar, a thief and a junkie*".

Issac went on to tell me that he had been smart enough to have borrowed cash on his father's credit cards before he'd left New York. He lived in a one-bedroom apartment in West Hollywood. He found a job as a shipping clerk in a warehouse but got fired after a short time for not 'spying' on the other warehouse employees, who were under suspicion of stealing merchandise.

After a month had passed, Issac was still jobless. He decided to use his bank automatic teller card to withdraw $100 ostensively so that he could continue his job search the next day.

"I drove down to the bank at 10 p.m. that night. I parked on the bank parking lot, about 30 yards in front of the automatic teller window. As I was walking toward the window I realized that the lone customer at the window was a drug dealer from my neighborhood. The bank window was secluded and the shrubbery blocked the view to the street. I stood back in the shadows and watched. I decided it was more economical for me to use his money than to deplete my nominal account. After all, it's not like robbing a decent person. He was a drug dealer."

"This drug dealer was about 5'8" and 140 pounds, and I'm at least two inches taller and 20 pounds heavier. My only concern was that I didn't want this guy to see my face, especially since we knew each other."

Issac went on to tell me how he perpetrated his first ATM robbery.

"I thought to myself that my best shield would be to attack him from the rear, and immediately drape his own jacket over his face. I hadn't time to second guess this strategy, as my prey was approaching. I backed deeper into the shadows, and as he passed me he was still counting his money with his head down. I stepped out of my hiding place, and took a quick glance around. I launched into the back of my victim, knocking him face first to the ground. I grabbed the tail of his three-quarter length jacket and pulled it over his head. I quickly positioned myself in such a way that my knees were on his coattail, pinning him to the ground."

"I lied when I told him that I had a gun pointed at the back of his head, and if he made a sound or moved a muscle he would die on the spot. I muffled my voice by covering my mouth with one hand. I took the cash from his hands and searched all his pockets. His cash withdrawal was $200, and his pockets produced another $80. After I took his watch and two rings, I told him to lie there until he said his prayers very slowly ten times. I walked casually back to my car and drove off."

"When I got back to my apartment, I gave some serious thought about the potential of a career robbing ATM customers. The next day I stayed home to think. That day I designed a mask from an old, white T-shirt. I sewed the neck closed and put two eye holes in the chest. At 10 p.m. that night, I drove back to the same bank branch and waited for another victim."

"I parked my car in the next block and walked back and took cover in the shrubbery near the automatic teller window. The first customer was a gay guy wearing earrings, lipstick and women's shoes. He wasn't driving or, at least, he didn't park in the bank parking lot. From my position I could watch him make his withdrawal and pocket his cash. He had to pass me on his way to the street. I slipped on my mask, withdrew my 10" butcher knife, and waited. As he walked within five feet of me I stepped from the bushes, grabbed him by the shirt and demanded all his cash, as I put the point of my knife on his neck. He didn't resist but pleaded with me not to hurt him and if his $60 wasn't enough he would withdraw more. He was so scared that I didn't even have to escort him back to the window. I told him to return with more money and if he ran I would shoot him in the back. (I lied). He told me that he could only withdraw $200 per day, but when he returned from the window he paid me the $140 balance. He thanked me several times for not hurting him. I did let him go unharmed."

"My new daily activity no longer included trips to the state employment office to see what jobs were available. Instead, I drove around West Hollywood in search of banks with automatic tellers windows. The windows that were difficult to see from the street were my ideal target. One night, while staking out an automatic teller window from a phone booth half a block away, I decided not to rob only gay men anymore. This was a business decision. A car pulled up in front of the bank. An older woman exited the passenger side, while the driver waited. I had to pass on this because the driver stayed in the car, and the window was in clear view of the driver. However, if the driver had gone to the window also, I could easily have robbed them both, plus taken their car."

"A few minutes later another woman approached the window. She seemed to be in her early 20's and a pedestrian. Nonetheless, I gave no thought to robbing her, for fear of the ferocious looking 'german sherman' at the other end of the short, thick dog chain she carried. After she finished her transaction, the dog pulled her in my direction, passed the phone booth, and yanked her on around the corner. I was tremendously relieved that she didn't want to use the phone."

"When I returned my attention to the bank, I saw a pick-up truck had parked there. There was no one inside the truck and a lone, middle-aged man at the window. This way my chance. I exited the phone booth and hurried down the street. When I got within a few feet in back of him, I took a last glance around, to make sure I saw no police cars or witnesses. Then I slipped on my T-shirt-mask, and pulled my knife from my waistband. Just as I was about to grab him from behind he turned around. He looked horrified and opened his mouth to scream, but I immediately covered his mouth with my free hand and pushed him hard against the bank building. I put my knife to his throat and demanded all his money. He gave me everything from his pockets, wallet, and his withdrawal. I asked him for his truck keys and he told me they were in the ignition. I told him I was going to take his truck and if he didn't object I would park it two blocks away, on the side street. However, if he did object I would have to stab him to death and I would take the truck anyway. I ordered him to remain at the window as if making a transaction until he saw the truck turn the corner, and then he was to walk calmly down the street to retrieve his pick-up. I drove the few blocks and parked his truck."

"After that first non-gay robbery, the rest came easy. I had to expand my activities to surrounding cities because the Hollywood and West Hollywood banks as well as community newspapers had begun to print warning notices about the *Automatic Teller Bandit*."

"It was strange, I'd robbed about 20 gay bank customers and the crimes never made TV or radio news. Now, after just a few heterosexual robberies, there was practically a county-wide manhunt. The police started using undercover cops as decoys at automatic bank tellers as bait. I had to change my method of operation to throw them off. So I began to wear different masks and disguises. Sometimes I would wear no disguise at all except dark glasses and a cap. There seemed to be many more bandits than there actually were. There were other automatic teller robbery specialists, but not nearly as many as it appeared. The police crack down was effective, the copy cats were getting busted right and left, night after night. I decided to lay low for awhile."

ROBBERY SCAM #4
Armed Robbery at the Mall

I continued my conversations with Issac O. and learned about the Mall Scam. Pay attention to this one. Since almost everyone goes to a mall sometime, almost everyone is a potential armed robbery victim.

Issac told me that while he was laying low, he developed his mall robbery techniques.

"Once while I was in a shopping mall having lunch, and watching the thousands of people hustling and bustling past, a money-making scheme came to me. I began to observe that there were twice as many women shopping as men. And women carried more packages than men, which meant they came prepared to spend more money. I decided to study the shopping habits of women."

"I followed ladies through the mall to determine which female group spent the most cash versus credit card purchases. I discovered more older women like to shop before five o'clock and more young women are evening shoppers. Older women like to shop with friends and wear more jewelry than younger women. Younger women are more apt to have children with them and be casually dressed."

"For the next two months I travelled daily to various shopping malls collecting data. I discovered sales on household items attracts more older women. Big sales on clothing attract more younger women. Month-end sales attract both equally. When women shopped with children or men they spent less money and left the mall sooner."

"Women shoplifters are usually middle-aged and well-dressed. Their favorite item to steal was cosmetics. During this research I witnessed ten women shoplifting, none were caught. Older women park their car closer to the store, and are more likely to leave the parking lot and shop elsewhere if more convenient parking space is available. Young women usually shop through lunch, while older women will take a lunch break. I gathered more information, and all this data was carefully studied."

"Finally, my new robbery specialty was decided. I would rob older women, in the parking lot of shopping malls. The women would have to be travelling in small groups. This way I would collect much more cash, and in the security of a small group. With a single friend, the women would be less likely to fear great bodily harm and suffer a heart-attack."

"I would always strike in the mornings, and only on days a major department store was having a big sale. And I would always strike before any of the victims exited the cars. This would attract less attention, plus reduce the risk of anyone screaming or running for help. I decided a knife would be more effective, because if I ever really had to hurt someone, no noise would be heard."

"My method of operation would be to park my car one block away from the street entrance, and walk to the parking area through the department stores. Then casually walk through the parking area as if going to my car and, if my research findings held up, my ideal victims would drive in every two minutes between nine and eleven a.m."

"I would linger close to where they were parking, as if I were searching my pockets for my keys. When the driver turned off her motor, I would let her get the door open before I struck. I planned to say something that would arouse her interest, like ask if this was the day of the half-price sale at J.C. Penney. The Sunday newspapers were full of sale ads for the upcoming Easter holiday."

According to Issac O. everything worked according to his plan. He worked his mall robbery scam for eight months and collected $95,000 in cash and jewelry.

"The robbery techniques I used were perfect. I never had to hurt anyone and I was never nearly captured. As my robberies became notorious, as usual, out came the copy cats. They were stabbing, beating and shooting their parking lot victims. And the copy cats didn't discriminate; any shopper, male, female, rich poor, young, old, alone or in a group, day or night were their potential victims. All this random crime disgusted me. Because of them, I was forced to lay low at the most lucrative time of the year. Damn copy cats."

THE OUTCOME

What finally happened to Issac O.? He told me that one day as he was patiently waiting in line at an ATM, he was recognized as the ATM robber by another customer waiting in line. He was arrested and eventually convicted of two counts of robbery and sentenced to ten years in state prison.

TIPS AGAINST CRIME

Here are Issac O's tips to reduce your risk of mall or ATM robbery.

- When you're travelling by car or truck, always be aware of your surroundings when your vehicle is stopped. Many street robbers specialize in motorists. Any neighborhood or motorist is vulnerable to this crime. Sometimes the would-be robber will involve you in a minor traffic accident to get you to exit your vehicle. And while you're exchanging information about the accident, they're subtly waiting for the most opportune moment to rob you.

  The would-be robbers usually select you by the type of car you are driving. The newer or more expensive the car, the more of a target you become. Your risk of this type of robbery increases if you are female, alone, elderly, (male or female), or appear intoxicated.

- When you're in a car, periodically check around you to see if the same car is behind, in front or on the side of you, for a long period of time. Even if a car is a couple cars behind you, if it persists, a red warning flag should go up in your mind. Don't panic. Your safety depends on it. In this case, simply make an unscheduled turn. If the vehicle continues to follow you, circle the entire block. By now the car should be gone. If not, proceed to the first open gas station or public place and stop. If you still see the car following you tell someone to alert the police and point your finger conspicuously at the vehicle. Then regardless of what happens, use a pay phone and tell someone of the experience. If possible give the license number and a complete description of the vehicle and passengers. Wait for the police to arrive.

When you're travelling by car or truck, always be aware of your surroundings when your vehicle is stopped.

- In the event that you're involved in a minor traffic accident, alone at night in a secluded area, and you suspect the accident may be a set-up, don't exit your car. Be prepared for such a situation. Have your name, insurance carrier and employment or home phone number pre-written and in your glove compartment inside a small envelope.

If a suspicious situation presents itself, lock all doors and windows before the other driver reaches your car. Tell them that you've a hospital emergency and must be on your way. However, this is where you may contact me, and slip the envelope through the barely cracked window. Then leave the scene as quickly as possible.

Men are especially vulnerable to this ploy when the other driver is a woman. Her accomplices may be hidden in the vehicle or nearby. When you leave the scene of an unreported accident after giving accurate information to the other party, this exempts you of hit and run. Before you leave write down the license plate number of the car, don't bother about seeing the other motorists drivers' license.

- Another method of robbing a motorist is to simply rush his/her car on foot, while the car is stopped at a traffic signal. The robber will usually select an easy target. That would be someone on a side street, and alone, with all their windows down or doors unlocked. Therefore, whenever you drive anywhere but especially on side streets, drive with all doors locked and windows

---

In the event that you're involved in a minor traffic accident, alone at night in a secluded area, and you suspect the accident may be a set-up, don't exit your car.

up. If any stranger appears to approach your car on foot, immediately become suspicious, and get out of there as quickly and safely as possible.

• In parking lots of shopping malls, motorists should be suspicious of any stranger approaching their car. Don't exit your car if a stranger seems to be standing or loitering uncomfortably close. Sound your horn if approached. Always park as close to the store as possible, and always inspect your car by looking in the front and back seat before getting back in.

• If you frequently shop at a particular shopping center, call their general office and ask about parking lot security. If they say that there is none, you and a few friends should insist that changes be made. Consult with your local police department, robbery division, to establish exactly how rampant parking lot robberies are in the shopping centers or mall in your area. Whether these findings are astronomical or minute, if your shopping place has inadequate parking lot security, public awareness should be raised. You and a small group of concerned citizens should solicit the support of other shoppers. Station yourselves at various locations throughout the mall and distribute fliers informing the shoppers of the robbery risks. Ask them to write letters to the plaza management, asking for more parking lot security, and they should sign their names to your petition demanding better security. Placard the surrounding community with notices asking other residents to join your crusade.

Whenever you drive anywhere, but especially on side streets, drive with all doors locked and windows up.

Present your suggestions for increased security to the general managers of the shopping plaza and also the local community newspaper. Suggestions should include surveillance cameras monitoring parking lots, patrolling security guards and a check and balance system to assure that motorist entering parking lots have safely entered the shopping center.

/

Chapter 3

Larceny Scams

The FBI defines larceny-theft as "the unlawful taking, carrying, leading, or riding away of property from the possession...of another." This crime category includes; shoplifting, picking pockets, purse-snatching, theft from motor vehicles, including motor vehicle parts and accessories, bicycle thefts, etc. It does not include embezzlement, "con-games", forgery, and worthless checks.

So what are some common larceny-theft scams?

LARCENY-THEFT SCAM #1:
Watch Out for the Mice

A 19-year-old of Arabic descent, currently serving a ten year sentence for vehicular manslaughter, and known by fellow convicts only by his nickname of 'Panther', says pickpocketing was his chief source of income from the day he ran away from an abusive home at the age of eight until he was arrested and sent to prison at eighteen. Panther told me that outdoor social functions are the premium of all possible venues for pick-pocketing. Activities such as amusement parks, circuses, carnivals, parades, all sporting events, political rallies, protest marches, concerts, etc. are ideal pick-pocketing opportunities. But crowded closed-in quarters are not the choice of professional pickpockets.

"In such places," Panther explains, "you're trapped if your victim finds out." He goes on to say that the prudent pickpocket artist avoids putting himself in an uncompro-

> *Be aware that outdoor social functions are the premium of all possible venues for pick-pocketing.*

mising position. "Open-air pickin's are the choice of the wise. You don't want to pickpocket a person and remain in close quarters with that person for any length of time. However, when I was nine years old," adds Panther, "I used to work with my unofficial adoptive parents as a decoy with my buddy, their son, Rat. He was younger than me. Rat's parents were professional pickpockets and they trained Rat and myself in the art. On crowded buses and elevators is where we applied our art best, with the use of Rat's pet mice." Rat's parents, Mr. and Mrs. Tarron, [not their real names of course] would take their son with them to buildings, major department stores, etc. Rat would carry with him his school lunch box and a couple of library books. Inside the lunch box would be two or three mice. When they got into the building they would pretend not to know each other and wander their separate ways.

The way their rip-off was planned, the three of them would eventually end up on the same crowded elevator, and when the elevator was between floors, going down, Rat would unlatch his lunch pail (supposedly by accident) and the mice would fall to the floor. With many women on the elevator, this would create a screaming chaotic frenzy, including that of Mrs. Tarron. The men would also become unnerved when my buddy would yell, 'Don't nobody touch them, they haven't been given their rabies shots'. While Rat scrambled on the floor, in the moving elevator, to capture his mice, Mrs. Tarron screamed and moved about pressing against the male passengers. She then pick-pocketed a couple of men and passed her take to Mr. Tarron before the doors opened.

By that time everything was a mess. The exact outcome was always unpredictable, except for a lucrative afternoon. Sometimes women would faint, mice would be trampled or stomped to death and some would escape down a corridor or through a crowded store but usually, Rat would get them back. Mr. Tarron would always be the first to leave the scene. Mrs. Tarron and Rat would leave in separate directions.

Panther went on to explain that he and his adopted family would execute their escaped-mice scam on crowded buses. The buses would be selected by their destination. If a bus was en route to a major sporting event, race track, or amusement park, it would be packed to standing room only capacity with customers carrying lots of cash. Those buses were targeted, says Panther.

"We would station ourselves a few feet from each other. Either Rat or I would have the lunch pail of mice. After a while, we'd let the mice loose. Mice would begin climbing over feet. Usually someone would scream, 'There're mice on this bus!' Then," Panther explains, "everybody would start pushing and shoving and brushing bodies against bodies. Mr. Tarron would be carrying a shopping bag half filled with rumpled newspapers. Mrs. Tarron and her two pick-pocketing partners would then subtly drop wallets into Mr. Tarron's bag. They would all exit at the next bus stop."

LARCENY-THEFT SCAM #2:
Theft at the Check Cashing Store

Young children are often a real asset to a pick-pocketing team. Panther went on to tell me that the Tarrons would often use the boys to set-up the "mark". Customers at banks and check cashing stores were especially vulnerable to being robbed by a team of professionals. He told me of one particular instance which should put everyone withdrawing cash from a bank or check cashing store on notice.

> *"Customers at banks and check cashing stores were especially vulnerable to being robbed by a team of professionals."*

"Mrs. Tarron would be inside watching the transactions while waiting in line to ask for change for a fifty, or a calendar, or a credit card application, any misleading question. When she spotted a man pocketing a good sum of cash she would follow him out of the building. Rat and I would already be outside running around, playing games with each other. We always pretended not to be acquainted with Mrs. Tarron, however, we always watched her every move for our signal. She would 'mark' our victim by removing a handkerchief from her handbag and coughing into it while pointing out our victim with her head and eyes."

"When we received this signal, Rat and I would run laughing in the direction of this mark. When we were within a few yards of him our playing would turn serious and a well-staged fist fight would start. We would really be going at each other when Mrs. Tarron came running and pleading with us to break it up. She would try to separate us while pleading for help. The mark would run over to give her assistance. We would be yelling and kicking at each other and trying hard to break loose. The prisoner of Mrs. Tarron would always break loose and rush the prisoner of our 'Good Samaritan."

"Now the 'mark' has two fighting boys on his hands to restrain. He's now surrounded by three professional pickpockets struggling, shouting, fighting, and keeping him off balance. Rat's mother would then zero in on the pocket holding the prize. When she has secured the loot (which only takes a matter of seconds) she covertly passes the take to Mr. Tarron who had just hurried over to assist. Now when Rat and Panther supposedly realize they can't win against two men, they agree to break up the fighting and shake hands. When the fight is over, Rat and I run down the street, Mrs. Tarron goes to her car, the 'mark' goes his way and Mr. Tarron (the come-lately stranger) continues on foot in another direction."

LARCENY-THEFT SCAM #3:
Good Pickin's at the Park

Panther continued recounting his experiences for me with this amusement park tale. Again, we all visit such parks, especially in the summer months. Pay attention to this scenario and see just how easy it is for a professional to separate you from your money.

"In the summer months the Tarrons worked the amusement parks. It was easy to choose a 'mark' because everywhere you looked you saw patrons extracting and depositing cash in purses and wallets. Mr. Tarron was an expert at lifting a gentlemen's wallet from his back pocket as the 'mark' fired air rifles and pellet guns at the shooting gallery."

"All the shooter's attention would be on hitting his target and winning a prize for his onlooking family, friends, or date. Mr. Tarron would position himself directly behind his victim and hope the man succeeded at his goal. If the shooter missed his target, Mr. Tarron wouldn't pick his pocket because the determined contestant may immediately reach for his wallet to pay for another opportunity. However, if the man won a big prize, the moment to strike would be just when the crowd got loud and everyone was congratulating him. Plus, there was little chance that he would immediately pay for another round. Mrs. Tarron would always be promptly on the scene to accept the pass. They would brush against each other briefly and in that split second, Mrs. Tarron would be in possession of the 'mark's' wallet and be proceeding in the opposite direction from the accomplice. After they ripped off ten or twelve victims, Mr. and Mrs. Tarron would relax and enjoy the festivities. An hour or so before closing the Tarrons would put Rat and I to work."

LARCENY-THEFT SCAM #4:
Sick at the Amusement Park

"The signal for us to go to work would be, *It's time to say our goodbyes.* Mrs. Tarron usually worked with me," says Panther, "and Mr. Tarron usually chose Rat. Rat and I would wander off in separate directions with our adult partner following close behind. What we would be looking for would be an easy mark. A person that seemed to be alone. Rat and I always looked for victims of the opposite sex of our partners. Since I worked with Mrs. Tarron, our ideal victim would be a man, and Rat's ideal victim would be a woman."

Panther explained, "I would spot an unaccompanied man and follow him for a few minutes to find out where he kept his wallet and whether or not it was fastened to his belt or pants. If the billfold wasn't attached, which is most often the case, I would position myself within a few feet from my intended victim and begin to conspicuously stagger blindly. When I was positive I had his attention, I would stand still for a moment and sway back and forth, as if about to faint."

"The 'mark' would observe this obviously ill little boy and approach sympathetically, wondering if I was sick. I'd coax him into escorting me to a nearby place to sit. With my arms around his waist, lifting his wallet would be easy. Then Mrs. Tarron would walk by, passing within inches. At that moment, I'd drop the wallet into her bag. In the rare event the wallet hadn't been lifted by the time our partner made his/her pass, he/she would immediately offer assistance to the ill child and the unattached stranger. Using charm and sex appeal the partner would distract our intended victim, providing a better opportunity to relieve the Good Samaritan of our prize. When the wallet had been taken, I would miraculously get better and excuse myself, to be reunited with my parents. Mrs. Tarron would linger behind with the unaware victim, flirting and keeping his mind busy until I was out of sight. Then Mrs. Tarron would excuse herself to be reunited with her spouse, which, she explains, she had been in search of at the time she had offered her assistance."

LARCENY-THEFT SCAM #5:
The Sports Arena Job

Crowds become especially loud and focussed at large scale sporting events. If you enjoy these type of outings, you are particularly vulnerable to pick-pockets. Panther explained to me just how his team would operate at such events.

"The four of us wander around continuously waiting for those climactic outbursts of excitement: the photo-finish, the home run, the touchdown, the slam dunk, the knock-out, etc. At that moment, when the crowd is on its feet, cheering and jumping up and down, that's the moment we strike. And before the excitement dies down we've vacated the area. In the rest room we remove all cash from the wallets and discard everything else. Then we wander to another area and wait for the next explosion."

LARCENY-THEFT SCAM #6
Grab-n-Run

As Panther got older, he and his buddy, Rat, began to work independently of Mr. and Mrs. Tarron. At twelve and thirteen years old they were a notorious purse snatching duo. They preyed on women walking alone, to or from their

---

"At that moment, when the crowd is on its feet, cheering and jumping up and down, that's the moment we strike."
—Panther

cars, in parking lots of supermarkets, banks, malls, and beauty salons.

"We had been taught by Mrs. Tarron that these were some of the prime times when women were most likely to be carrying money in their purses, versus intimate places underneath their clothing. Her reasoning, I suppose, was that you never see a woman reach underneath her clothing to pay for her groceries, hairdo, or make bank deposits."

"But snatching a woman's purse as she walks down the street or waits at a bus stop is taking two unnecessary risks. First of all, she may not have any money with her, and secondly, if she does, it's only a fifty-fifty chance the money is in her purse. So we chose our victim by several factors: (1) If she didn't have a shoulder strap attached to her body that was connected to the purse; (2) If she held the purse with one hand, swinging it at her side; (3) If her walking pace was slow; (4) If she was with a small child; or (5) If she was fat, handicapped, or elderly. Our well-selected victim would have to meet at least two of our prerequisites plus be in a parking lot or entering a beauty salon before we would give her the dubious award of our mastery."

"My preferred method of snatching a purse," explains Panther, "would be to creep up on a victim from the rear. Whenever I'd strike in such a fashion, I would run the opposite direction to avoid the victim ever seeing my face. I would always try to be within a few blocks of a bus depot, bus driver rest stop, or a taxi stand, to ensure me fast evacuation from that vicinity. Purse snatching was a short-lived profession for Rat and myself. It was entirely too much running, and being chased by Good Samaritans, too many close calls for our style."

"My preferred method of snatching a purse would be to creep up on a victim from the rear."
—Panther

LARCENY-THEFT SCAM #7:
Shoplifting

"Shoplifting was a more honorable profession for a teenage thief. It required more finesse, and a degree of artistry, unlike what I came to consider barbaric purse snatching. My adoptive family was relieved and proud of their two son's choices to abandon their purse snatching careers for something that held more of a future. Between our pick-pocketing and shoplifting, my brother and I accumulated enough income to both buy new cars at the age of sixteen. We mostly stole costume jewelry and sold it to our elite teenage friends and classmates."

Some Facts About Shoplifting

Shoplifting is a form of larceny or theft. It is the crime of taking goods from a store without payment or the intent to pay. Some states have a separate punishable crime called *concealment.* This law prohibits you from putting any items into pockets or bags before you pay for them. As soon as you remove the item from plain sight you may be legally arrested. This crime is an attempted shoplifting. Saying 'But I intended to pay for it when I reached the cashier' is a futile excuse.

Any form of store theft is shoplifting. This involves theft by employees and also business partners that take merchandise home without paying for, or making a record of, the item removed.

According to the 1988 Uniform Crime Reports, about one in seven larcenies reported to law enforcement is for shoplifting.

> *Teens are more likely than any other age group to shoplift. They are about twice as likely as members of the adult population, to be shoplifters.*

There are four different types of shoplifters;

1) Kleptomaniacs - people who have a mental disor-
der and cannot overcome a compulsion to steal.
2) Amateurs - people who steal on impulse because
they see an item they want.
3) Professional shoplifters (often called 'Boosters') -
people who make their living stealing from different
stores.
4) Drug addicts and other desperate people - those
who steal to obtain money for other habits or
personal problems.

Teens are more likely than any other age group to
shoplift. Teen shoplifters are about equally divided
between the sexes. Women between ages eighteen and fifty
are the second most likely group to shoplift, according to
most studies. Senior citizens are the least likely group to
shoplift.

Most things the amateur shoplifter takes don't have
much dollar value. In fact, the average take is about $42.
Still, shoplifting is a multi-billion dollar industry. And
small businesses feel the loss more than large department
stores. The following tips require prudence and ingenuity,
but cost little to ensure that your merchandise remains in
the store until properly purchased:

TIPS AGAINST CRIME

Here are tips to guard against shoplifters.

1) Alert employees are a great defense. They should
greet customers when they enter the store. They should be

---

*Teens are three times likely as persons over age 65 to be tar-
gets for thieves.*

taught to be attentive, in a tactful manner. All employees should be instructed that excessive shoplifting from the store, or their department, will jeopardize their job security. A procedure for deterring shoplifting should be established, and all employees should comply. Routine anti-theft meetings should be held.

2) Make sure you can see everything that goes on in your store. Keep counters low, no more than waist high. Mount mirrors in corners so there are no blind spots.

3) Make it hard to leave your store without paying. Place expensive items in the center of the store, away from exits.

4) Arrange counters and display tables so there's no direct route to the exit. Some stores put turnstiles at entrance so the only way to get out is through the checkout counter.

5) Arrange your displays so that missing items are easily noticed. Place small items in neat rows or clearly defined patterns. If you must, fasten expensive merchandise and attach alarms.

6) Announce and observe a policy to prosecute shoplifters. The threat of being caught, questioned by police, put on trial, and maybe even in jail, may deter most shoplifters. When a shoplifter is caught, always prosecute if they're 12 years old or older. Under 12 years old (at your own discretion) rather than calling the police, arrange a meeting with a parent. But only the first time. Next time, prosecute. An empty threat is meaningless.

If the attacker is only after your purse or other valuables, don't resist. *You don't want to escalate a property crime into a violent confrontation.*

7) If shoplifting gangs are a problem in your neighborhood, organize a *Merchant's Alert Program*. When you spot a gang "working" your store, notify your colleagues, so they will be on alert.

8) Offer small awards to teenagers and other youngsters that can help you with creative ideas to reduce shoplifting.

LARCENY-THEFT SCAM #8:
Pick-Pockets and Hotel Suites

The Tarron Clan ripped-off unsuspecting victims throughout the year, says Panther, but their business flourished during the vacation circuit. "At a particular point in our eight state tour, we were in St. Louis, Missouri, staying in luxury hotels. Our standard procedure was to reserve a luxury suite well in advance whenever possible. When we arrived, we would register at the desk and adjourn to our quarters. Mr. Tarron always travelled with a portable key cutting machine. Once the bellhop left our suite, Mr. Tarron would duplicate the door key. And within five minutes, he would be on the phone to the front desk complaining about the room (i.e, the view is not what he expected, his wife hates blue carpet, he would like a larger suite, or a smaller suite) and, eventually, we would be re-registered in another room or suite. Of course Dad retained the duplicate key for posterity."

"On this occasion, our previous suite had been the Presidential Suite and it was enormous. And it's new tenants were a group of foreign businessmen, nine to be exact. The Tarrons gave Rat and myself turns at robbing our previous hotel rooms. This hotel was mine. Throughout the day we hit all the tourist attractions as a family and perpetrated our pick-pocketing trade. At night our parents worked the night clubs as a couple, and it was the selected sons assignment to figure out the optimum moment to accomplish his mission."

"For three consecutive nights I had telephoned the Presidential Suite from a pay phone in the lobby. And for three consecutive nights there was always someone present to answer their phone."

"However, on the fourth night about 11:30 p.m. I received a phone call in our suite. It was Mrs. Tarron phoning from the lobby. She told me she thought she would give me a tip, all my 'friends' were in the club enjoying a two hour stage show. I got dressed in dark clothes, sneakers and gloves, and left our room on the 8th floor and took the elevator to the 12th floor. When I reached their door I knocked a couple of times as a precaution, although I had just telephoned to the unoccupied suite two minutes earlier. I entered with my key and began to search for cash, credit cards, and jewelry. I was only in the suite for 30 seconds when I heard a key entering the front door. Quickly, I rolled my body under the nearby King-sized bed. It was three of the men. They sat in the dining area and began to play poker. Hours had passed when the other six men arrived. Some watched TV and some went to bed, and some played cards. By 3:45 a.m. they were all asleep. Two slept with their heads laying on the dinette table, one in a reclining chair, and one on one of the three sofas, and both King-sized beds were occupied."

"I crawled and prowled through the entire suite, searching all the luggage, the closets, and drawers, the clothing lying around, and pick-pocketed the two fully clothed men asleep at the table. When I tip-toed from their hotel suite at 4:30 a.m., the pillow slip I brought with me was ten pounds heavier. Mom, Dad and my brother, Rat, were still sitting up in their pajamas, playing monopoly, when I entered the room. We stayed up celebrating my victory until 7:00 a.m. It was our biggest take from any single hotel suite."

THE OUTCOME

Although Panther's criminal career extended a decade, he was never once arrested. However, on his Prom night he had been smoking dope and drinking heavily. While driving to another after-hours Prom-night party, Panther was in a fatal auto accident. The two female passengers in his vehicle as well as his adopted brother Rat were killed. The other driver sustained major injuries to the head and back, but survived. Panther is serving a ten year sentence for vehicular manslaughter.

TIPS AGAINST CRIME

Most thieves are looking for things that are easy to grab and easy to keep or sell without anyone asking questions. Three rules can reduce your chances of being a victim.

1 Keep track of your belongings. Don't leave them. Someone could easily pick them up; like in an empty classroom, the front yard, porch, the seat of a car.

2 Don't flash your cash or brag about your valuables.

3. Put your name or initials on your property. Use an indelible marker, stickers, name tags, or an engraving tool. You can ask your police department or Neighborhood Watch group for help.

Here are Panther's tips to guard against pick-pockets and purse snatchers.

* When walking, never drift aimlessly along. Always walk with a pace and posture of authority. Choose well-lighted, busy streets and avoid passing vacant lots, alleys, or construction sites. Take the long way if it's the safest way.

* Know your neighborhood. Find out what stores and restaurants are open late and where the police and fire-stations are.

• Carry your purse close to your body and keep a firm grip on it. Carry a wallet in an inside coat pocket or side trouser pocket, not in the rear trouser pocket.

• Don't flaunt expensive jewelry or clothing.

• Walk facing traffic so you can see approaching cars.

• Don't overburden yourself with packages and groceries that make it hard for you to react. Have your car or house key in hand as you approach your vehicle or home.

• If you suspect you're being followed by someone on foot, cross the street and head for the nearest well-lit, populated area. Walk quickly, or run to a house or store to call the police. If you are really scared, scream for help.

• When travelling in buses and subways, don't fall asleep. Stay alert!

• In the subway, stand back from the platform edge. Avoid sitting near the exit door. An attacker can reach in and grab a purse or jewelry as the train pulls away.

• While waiting, stand with other people or near the token or information booth. You are a less likely purse-snatching victim surrounded by possible Good Samaritans.

• Be alert to who gets off the bus or subway with you. If you feel uncomfortable, walk directly to a place where there are other people.

• Drive with all the car doors locked. Keep windows closed whenever possible. Never pick up hitchhikers.

• If you see another motorist in trouble, signal that you will get help and then go phone the police.

• If your car breaks down, raise the hood, use flares, or tie a white cloth to the door handle. Stay in the locked car. When someone stops, ask them to phone for help.

• Park in well-lit areas that will still be well-lit when you return. Lock your doors.

• Be particularly alert and careful when using underground and enclosed parking garages.

• If you are being followed while driving, drive to the nearest police or fire station, open gas station, or other business, or well-lighted residence where you can safely call police. Try to get the car's license number and description. If no safe areas are near, honk the horn repeatedly and turn on your emergency flashers.

ON BUSES AND SUBWAYS:

• Try to use well-lit and frequently used stops.
• Try to sit near the bus driver. Take a seat in the subway car near the conductor.
• If you are verbally or physically harassed, attract attention by talking loudly or screaming.

IN ELEVATORS:

- Look in the elevator before getting in to be sure no one is in hiding.
- Stand near the controls.
- Get off if someone suspicious enters. If you're worried about someone who is waiting for the elevator with you, pretend you forgot something and don't get on.
- If you are attacked inside the elevator, hit the alarm and as many floor buttons as possible.

JOGGING, BIKING, etc:

- Choose routes in advance that are safe and well populated.
- Vary your route and schedule.
- Don't jog and bike at night.
- Know businesses that are open and locations of police and fire stations.
- Consider carrying a shriek alarm.
- Consider not wearing your stereo headphones. It's safer to be alert.

AT SCHOOL:

- Keep your locker locked. Use a good key instead of a combination lock if possible.
- Don't keep money or anything valuable in your locker, especially overnight, through the weekend, or over the holidays.
- Lock your bike with a case-hardened chain of cable and lock, winding the cable through the frame and both wheels and then around a bike rack or stationary object.

AT HOME:

- Make sure your house or apartment has a good key-operated deadbolt lock on the front and back doors. Always lock the door when you go out, even if it's just for a few minutes.
- Be careful with your house keys. Keep them with you and not in your school locker. Never have your name and address on the key ring.
- Don't hide keys outside the house. Thieves know all the good hiding places!
- Put your bike and any sports equipment inside the house, apartment, or garage at night.

OUT AND ABOUT:

- Don't leave your purse or wallet on the counter while you're looking at something in a store.
- Don't dangle or swing your purse by the straps. Try to carry it close to you, especially in crowded stores and streets. Keep a wallet in a side, not a back pocket.

HELP OTHERS:

- Be a good neighbor. When you're going to and coming from home and school, watch for strangers or suspicious activities. Tell your parents and the police about anything unusual. Don't tell a stranger that a neighbor is not home or lives alone.

Tips For Travelers

It's a fact that almost all types of personal and house-hold crime are highest in the warm months, when people spend more time away from home on vacations or are involved in outdoor activities. Avoid becoming part of this statistic by following these suggestions to protect your home, property, and family while you're relaxing and having fun. Before you leave use this checklist to secure your home.

- Make sure your home looks lived in, not empty: stop mail and cancel all deliveries, or ask a friend to make daily collections. Hide empty garbage cans. Leave shade and blinds in normal positions. Put an automatic timer on several lights and on the radio. Leave a TV on, put a timer on it to remain on when the radio is off. Have a neighbor keep your property maintained.
- Leave a key with a trusted neighbor.
- Store valuables in a safe deposit box.
- Tell a neighbor you trust your departure and return dates. Supply an itinerary with phone numbers where you can be reached in an emergency.
- Ask police if they have a "Vacation Home Check" program.
- Lock all windows and doors. Double-check basement and garage doors before you leave.
- Put burglar alarm and neighborhood watch decals on several windows of your home.

WHILE TRAVELING:

- Carry a minimum amount of cash. Use travelers' checks and credit cards, but keep a record of their numbers in a separate and safe place.
- Never pick up hitchhikers.
- Don't advertise or brag about your plans.
- Keep careful tabs on your travel tickets. They're as good as cash. Carry them in an inside pocket, not protruding from a jacket or bag.

- Always lock your car when it's parked, even if the stop is brief. Keep valuables out of sight, preferably locked in the trunk. Don't leave wallet, checkbooks, or purses in the car, unless they are well hidden.
- If you stop overnight, remove bags and other valuables from the car and take them inside.
- If your car breaks down, turn on your flashers and raise the hood or tie a white cloth to the antenna. If you must abandon your car, keep all passengers together.
- Carry a flashlight with fresh batteries, a fire extinguisher, blankets for each passenger, nonperishable food, portable telephone or CB radio and first aid kit. If you legally possess a firearm, carry it   unloaded under your front seat with ammunition concealed within reach.
- Avoid travelling during the night hours if you can. If you are in a foreign country, learn the words for police officer and doctor. Know locations of the nearest United States Consulate.

MOTELS AND HOTELS:

- Check room for hidden intruder each time you enter.
- Arrange with the manager or front desk to inquire (by phone) as to your safety at least once daily. Especially if you're a woman travelling alone, whenever returning to your room at night first alert the desk clerk that you'll phone them when you've secured your room. If they don't hear from you in ten minutes, they should investigate.
- Use auxiliary locking devices when occupying or leaving your room.
- When an unexpected knock sounds at your door, and unless you're familiar with the visitor, don't

open your door until you first notify the front desk. If he claims to be 'room service' and you weren't expecting any, first ask for his name and the name of his supervisor, then verify his presence by phone with the front desk.

• Keep extra cash and valuables locked in the hotel safe deposit box, not in the room. Always take cash, credit cards, and keys with you.

• Inventory your belongings daily.

• Be observant. Report any suspicious movements in the corridors or other rooms to the management.

What If It Happens To You?

Remain calm and try not to panic or show any signs of anger or confusion. If the attacker is only after your purse or other valuables, *don't resist*. You don't want to escalate a property crime into a violent confrontation.

Make a conscious effort to get an accurate description of your attacker: age, race, complexion, body build, height, weight, type and color of clothing.

Lastly, call the police immediately, identifying yourself and your location. Contact your local victim assistance agency to help deal with the trauma that all crime victims experience. They can also help you learn about victim compensation laws and how to follow your case's progress.

Chapter 4

Investment Scams

Interested in investing? Maybe you have a small sum saved up for your retirement and you want it to grow, at least a little, in the next few years before you retire? Or maybe you're just two thousand dollars short of a reasonable downpayment for a starter home and you would like to make your money grow just a bit faster than it does at your credit union? Why not go ahead and invest in the stock market? Because like most people, you're scared of what you don't understand and you're scared of getting scammed. Well, after you read this chapter, you should be familar with some of the more ingenious investment scams. Pay attention so that you're not the next victim. Knowledge is your most powerful frontline protection against these expert swindlers.

Americans are investors. We purchase stocks and bonds, contribute to savings programs, own real estate, participate in futures and options market, acquire collectibles, provide start-up capital for new business ventures, buy franchises, and loan money to relatives. The strength of our economy is in large measure the product of our combined investments.

Perhaps more so than any people in the world, we enjoy an ever-expanding variety of investments to choose from, coupled with the freedom to make our own investment decisions. Sometimes it's too much for us to take in and learn, but it's still our right to earn and lose at our discretion.

Unfortunately, some unscrupulous promoters abuse our freedom to choose by concocting investment schemes that have zero possibility of making money for anyone other than themselves. Such persons promise investment rewards they cannot possibly deliver and have no intention of delivering. They are swindlers. Many of them are very good at it. One estimate puts the annual loss to investment fraud at $10 billion. That's more money than the combined annual profits of the nation's three major auto makers!

Successful investment swindlers use every trick in the book, and some that aren't even recorded, to convince you that none of the descriptions and precautions in this chapter apply to them. After all, they are offering you a once-in-a-lifetime opportunity to make a lot of money quickly. Read on. You'll see some of their methods of gaining your trust are really ingenious.

Who Are The Investment Swindlers?

She is the sweet, friendly, caring voice on a telephone. Or a friend of a friend. They reach in and perform surgery on your savings from a dingy back office to an opulent hotel suite. They may have no apparent connection to the investment business or they may have an alphabet soup of impressive letters following their names. They may be glib and fast talking or so seemingly shy and soft-spoken that you feel almost compelled to force your ideas on them.

The first rule of protecting yourself from an investment swindle is to rid yourself of any notions you might have as to what an investment swindler looks like or sounds like. Indeed, some swindlers don't start out to be swindlers.

There are case histories in which individuals who held positions of trust and esteem—accountants, attorneys, bonafide investment brokers and even doctors—have sacri-

---

The first rule of protecting yourself from an investment swindle is to rid yourself of any notions you might have as to what an investmnet swindler looks like or sounds like.

ficed their ethics for the fast buck of running an investment scam.

In still other cases, investment programs that began with legitimate intentions went sour through happenstance or poor management, leading the promoter to mishandle or abscond with investors' capital. Whether an investment is planned as a scam or simply becomes one, the result is the same. Someone loses money or valuables.

This is why, as we will discuss, protecting your savings against fraud involves at least three steps: carefully checking out the person and firm you would be dealing with; taking a close and cautious look at the investment offer itself, and continuing to monitor the investment that you decide to make. None of these precautions alone may be sufficient.

Who Are The Victims of Investment Fraud?

If you are absolutely certain it could never happen to you, the investment swindler starts with a big advantage. Investment fraud generally happens to people who think it couldn't happen to them.

Just as there is no typical profile for swindlers, neither is there one for their victims. While some scams target persons who are known or thought to have deep pockets, most swindlers take the attitude that everyone's money spends the same. It simply takes more small investors to fund a large fraud. In fact, some swindlers deliberately seek out families that may have limited means or financial difficulties, figuring such persons may be particularly receptive to a proposal that offers fast and large profits.

> *Investment fraud generally happens to people who think it couldn't happen to them.*

Although victims of investment fraud can differ from one another in many ways, they do, unfortunately, have one trait in common: greed that exceeds their caution. Plus a willingness to believe what they want to believe. Movie actors and athletes, professional persons and successful business executives, political leaders and internationally famous economists have all fallen victim to investment fraud. So have hundreds of thousands of others, including widows, retirees and working people, people who made their money the hard way and lost it the fast way. Remember, your defenses are not impenetrable. It only takes the right scam and the right swindler and you've lost your nest egg.

How Investment Swindlers *Attract* Victims

Swindlers attempt to pitch the sales approaches of legitimate investment firms and sales persons. Thus the fact that they may contact you in a particular way - by phone, mail, or even through a referral - should not in itself be viewed as an indication that the investment is or isn't shady. Many totally reputable firms also use the same methods to effectively and economically identify individuals who may have an interest in their investment products and services.

Bearing in mind that to investigate before you invest is good advice no matter how you are approached, these are some of the methods con men commonly employ to contact their victims-to-be.

SCAM VEHICLE #1:   The Telephone: So-called telephone boiler-rooms remain a favorite way for swindlers and their sales squads to quickly contact large numbers of potential investors. Even if a swindler has to make 100 to 200 phone calls to find a mooch (one of the terms swindlers use for their victims), he figures that the opportunity to pocket thousands of dollars of someone's savings is still good pay for the time and cost involved.

SCAM VEHICLE #2:   US Mail: Some sellers of fraudulent investment deals buy bonafide mailing lists—names and addresses of persons who, for example, subscribe to a particular investment-related publication who have responded to previous direct mail offers, or who have other characteristics that swindlers find appealing. In the hope of avoiding notice by postal authorities, mail-order swindlers may not make a direct or immediate pitch for your money. Rather, they often seek to entice you to write or phone even if you didn't respond to the mailing.

SCAM VEHICLE #3:   Advertisements: A newspaper or magazine ad may offer (or at least hint at) profit opportunity far more attractive than available through conventional investments. Once you have taken the bait, the swindler will then attempt to "set the hook". Even though investment crooks know that regulatory agencies routinely monitor ads in major publications, some nevertheless use such publications in the hope of being able to hit-and-run before an investigator shows up. Others advertise in narrowly circulated publications that they think regulators are less likely to see.

SCAM VEHICLE #4:   Referrals: One of the oldest scams going involves paying fast, large profits to initial investors (from their own or other investors money) knowing that they are likely to recommend the investment to their friends. And these friends will tell their friends. Soon, the swindler no longer needs to find new victims.

SCAM VEHICLE #5: The "Reputable" Business: Some swindlers go first class. Using profits from previous swindles, they rent plush offices, hire an interior decorator and a professional sounding receptionist and open what has the appearance—but not the reality—of a reputable investment firm. You may even have to phone for an appointment, and once there, don't be surprised to be kept waiting (that's intended to make you all the more eager).

This kind of swindler's success depends on how long he can keep his victims from knowing they are being cheated. Investors are assured that their large profits are being reinvested to earn even larger profits. Such a swindler may join local civic groups, contribute to charities, and generally play the role of solid citizen.

Techniques Investment Swindlers Use

Their techniques are as varied as their methods of establishing contact. If there is a common denominator, however, it is their ability to be convincing. The skills that make them successful are essentially the same skills that enable any good salesperson to be successful. But, swindlers have a decided advantage: They don't have to make good on their promises. In the absence of such responsibility, they have no reluctance to promise whatever it takes to persuade you to part with your money. Here are a few of their more popular techniques:

SCAM TECHNIQUE #1: Expectation of Large Profits: The profits a swindler talks about are generally large enough to make you interested and eager to invest, but not so large as to make you overly skeptical. Or she may mention a profit figure she thinks you will consider believable and then, as a further enticement, suggest that the potential profit is actually far greater than that. The latter figure, of course, is the one she hopes you'll focus on. Generally speaking, if an investment proposal sounds too good to be true, it probably is.

SCAM TECHNIQUE #2: Low Risk: Some scammers are so blatant as to suggest there's no risk, that the investment is a sure moneymaker. Obviously, the last thing a swindler wants you to think about is the possibility of losing your money. (If you ask how you can be certain your money's safe, you can count on a plausible sounding answer. Besides, at this point, he figures you will believe what you 'want' to believe.) To make his pitch more credible, a swindler may acknowledge that there could be 'some' risk, then quickly assure you it's minimal in relation to the profits you will most certainly make.

A con man may become impatient or even aggressive if the question of risk is raised - perhaps suggesting that he has better things to do than waste time with people who lack the courage and foresight needed to make money! With this kind of put down, he hopes you won't bring up the subject again.

SCAM TECHNIQUE #3: Urgency: There's usually some compelling reason why it's essential for you to invest right now. Perhaps because the investment opportunity can *only be offered to a limited number of people*, or because delaying the investment could mean missing out on a large profit, after all, once the information he has confided to you becomes generally known, the price is sure to go up. Right?

Urgency is important to a swindler. For one thing, he wants your money as quickly as possible with a minimum of effort on his part. And he doesn't want you to have a chance to think it over, discuss it with someone who might suggest you become suspicious, or check him or his proposal out with a regulatory agency. Besides, he may not plan on remaining in town very long.

SCAM TECHNIQUE #4: Confidence: They don't call them con men (and women) for nothing! They sound so confident about the money you are going to make so that 'you' become confident enough to let go of your savings. Their message is that they are doing you a favor by offering you such a golden investment opportunity. A swindler may even threaten (pleasantly or otherwise) to end the discussion by suggesting that if you are not really interested there are many other people who will be. Once you protest that you are interested, he figures your savings are practically in his pocket.

Although you can't necessarily spot a con man or woman by the way he or she talks, most are strong willed, articulate individuals who will dominate the conversation, even if they do it in a low-key, friendly sort of way. The more they talk, the less chance you have to ask questions.

Investment Swindles And How They Work

There's a saying among swindlers that it's not the scam that counts, it's the sell. Judging from the number of arcane and often outlandish schemes that have been employed to separate otherwise prudent people from their money, the saying would seem to reflect reality. The evidence is that if people can be made believers, they can be sold practically anything. Consider several of the ways in which hustlers of phony investments have won the confidence of persons whom they planned to victimize.

INVESTMENT SCAM #1:
The Old-Fashioned Ponzi Scheme

It's become one of the oldest and most often employed investment schemes because it's proven to be one of the most lucrative. While there are innumerable variations, here's how a person we will call, Frank C., practiced it.

At the outset, Frank approached relatively small numbers of influential people in the community and offered them the opportunity to invest—with a guaranteed high return—in a computer-generated program of arbitrage in foreign currency fluctuations. To be sure, it sounded high-tech and sophisticated but Frank had his eye on sophisticated and well-heeled victims.

Within a short period of time, he approached and sold the scheme to still other investors, then promptly used a portion of the money invested by these persons to pay large profits to the original group of investors. As word spread of Frank's genius for making money and paying profits, even more would-be investors anxiously put up even larger sums of money. Some of it was used to recycle the fictitious profit payments and, like a pebble in the water, the word of fast and fabulous rewards produced an ever-widening circle of eager investors. And more money poured in. And Frank C., left town a wealthy man.

INVESTMENT SCAM #2:
The Infallible Forecaster

Jim L., (among his many aliases) had a full-time daytime job but, with assets that consisted only of a phone, patience, and an easy way of talking, he managed to parlee his nighttime sideline into a large, nevertheless ill-gotten fortune. The routine went like this:

Jim would phone someone we'll call Mrs. Smith and quickly assure her that, "No" he didn't want her to invest a single cent. "Never invest with someone you don't know," he preached. But he said he would like to demonstrate his firm's "research skills" by sharing with her the forecast that so-and-so commodity was about to experience a significant price increase. Sure enough, the price went up.

A second phone call didn't solicit an investment either. Jim simply wanted to share with Mrs. Smith a prediction that the price of so-and-so commodity was about to go down. "Our forecasts will help you decide whether ours is the kind of firm you might someday want to invest with," he added. As predicted, the price of the commodity subsequently declined.

By the time Mrs. Smith received a third call, she was a believer. She not only wanted to invest but insisted on it, with a big enough investment to make up for the opportunities she had already missed out on.

What Mrs. Smith had no way of knowing was that Jim had begun with a calling list of two hundred people. In the first call, he told one hundred people that the price of so-and-so commodity would go up and the other one hundred were told it would go down. When it went up, he made a second call to the one hundred who had been given the correct forecast. Of these, fifty were told the next price move would be up and fifty were told it would go down.

The end result? Once the predicted price decline occurred, Jim had a list of fifty people eager to invest. After all, how could they go wrong with someone so obviously infallible in forecasting prices?

But go wrong they did, the moment they decided to send Jim a half million dollars from their collective savings accounts.

INVESTMENT SCAM #3: All That Glitters...

Not only did the two brothers have a fancy office building with their own company name on it, but the investment offer seemed sound and straightforward: "Instead of buying gold outright and holding it for appreciation, make a small down payment that the firm could use to secure financing that would permit much larger quantities of gold to be bought and held for the investor's account." That way, when the price of gold rose—as was "sure to happen" —investors stood to realize highly leveraged profits.

The company provided storage vaults where investors could view the wall-to-wall stacks of glittering bullion. By the time the authorities caught wind of the scheme's suspicious smell and looked for themselves, it turned out the only thing gold was the color of the paint on the cardboard used to construct look-alike bars of bullion. The counterfeit gold, however, proved far easier to find than the millions of dollars of invested money.

* * *

Who to tell if you're a victim of a scam:

Federal Trade Commission
6th Street and Pennsylvania Avenue NW
Washington, DC   20580
Phone: (202) 326-3150

Housing and Urban Development Department, Interstate Land Sales Registration Building 451
7th Street SW, Room 6262
Washington, DC 20410
Phone: 1 (800) 755-0502

National Association of Securities Dealers
1735 K Street NW
Washington, DC   20006
Phone: (202) 729-8044

National Futures Association
200 W. Madison, Suite 1600
Chicago, IL 60606
Phone: 1 (800) 621-3570. In Illinois: 1 (800) 572-9400

Securities and Exchange Commission
450 Fifth Street
Washington, DC 20006
Phone: (202) 728-8233

United States Postal Service
Chief Postal Inspector
Room 3021,
Washington, DC 20260-2100
Phone: (202) 268-5267

Your local police.

Your local consumer protection agency.

*   *   *

Referrals:

American Association of Retired Persons (AARP) 1909 K Street NW, Washington DC 20049. Phone: (202) 728-4363. AARP operates a general crime prevention clearinghouse. They are recognized experts in the treatment of issues concerning the elderly.

Elder Abuse and Neglect Clearinghouse, CANE Exchange, College of Humane Resources, University of Delaware, Newark, DE. Phone:(302) 451-2301. New clearinghouse on information concerning elder abuse and neglect. Please write for additional information.

Chapter 5

Credit Scams

More and more companies have turned to the computer in order to make their operations more efficient. Unfortunately, as technology becomes more sophisticated, so do the criminals.

Computer crime has serious implications for business. In fact, losses from computer crime are estimated to be more than $555 million a year in the United States alone. Virtually any organization using a computer network is at risk. Consumers are affected also, their credit, medical, and financial records can be tapped, and they will probably have to bear the cost for security actions taken by the government and private industry.

Computer crimes can range from vandalism, especially in the form of computer viruses, to theft of services, information, and money. Although computer viruses account for only a small percentage of computer crime, the damage they can cause is enormous.

A computer virus is a program created to disrupt, damage, or even destroy your computer's operating programs or data. It can erase files from a floppy or hard disc, steal information, reformat a hard disc, even burn out a monitor. A *computer virus*, which was allegedly created by a student at Cornell University, shut down thousands of computers in the Internet network, at an estimated cost of $100 million to $300 million in lost time.

Virtually any organization using a computer network is at risk.

Theft of services is the fastest growing category of prosecuted computer crime. The most common goals of such crimes are theft of telephone or computer service, which can involve thousands of dollars.

Theft of money accounted for 36 percent of computer crimes in 1987. Often the theft is perpetrated by an insider, someone who has access to confidential information and passwords. However, anyone with a computer, a modem (a a device which connects one computer to another via telephone lines), and knowhow can gain entry. In 1989, Security Pacific Bank in Los Angeles lost $350,000 through illegal use of a card which gave the thief access to the automatic teller machine's computer system.

Part of the problem in controlling computer crime is that very few computer crimes are reported, and still fewer are prosecuted, according to the National Center for Computer Data. In addition, the laws which govern computer crime are not comprehensive enough to deal effectively with the increasingly sophisticated technology, say some computer experts and lawyers who specialize in computer crime.

Much of the responsibility for preventing computer crime will have to be assumed by those who are affected by it; namely, businesses and consumers. According to Larry Potts, of the FBI's white collar crime program, the only way to reduce computer crime is for businesses to improve security.

Safeguarding Your System

Imagine this scenario: You're preparing a detailed report for your company, when a computer virus strikes,

---

Much of the responsibility for preventing computer crime will have to be assumed by those who are affected by it; namely, business and consumers.

erasing all of your files and data. Weeks of work are irretrievably lost, and now you must work triple time to restore the information. Sound scary? Well, loss of time and information could be the least of your problems. But there are ways to protect your system from computer viruses. When it comes to viruses, prevention is the best medicine:

1) Always back up your data, and do it frequently. This way, if a virus destroys your files, you'll have relatively current copies. This is a good idea anyway, since it will also safeguard your system in the event of other kinds of computer failure.

Most people who work with computers on a daily basis say they backup data regularly. It's too bad that most of these regulars only get the picture after they lose their most important files.

2) Always put write-protect tabs on floppy discs that you aren't using to send or store data. These tabs are usually included with commercially packaged diskettes. If you get a message such as *Write protect error writing drive A* something is wrong, but the tab will protect your diskette.

3) Be wary of downloading (copying programs or information) from bulletin board systems. Use established systems which check the software they post. Before downloading a new program, wait a few weeks to see if any problems surface.

4) Don't lend your program discs to anybody. They may come back infected. If you must lend a copy, reformat it when it's returned.

Don't lend your program disks to anybody. They may come back infected. If you must lend a copy, reformat it when it's returned

5) If your system uses a floppy disc drive, use only one disc to boot up. Make sure the disc you use is write-protected. If you have a hard disc, don't boot from a floppy.

6) Avoid letting other people use your system; or at least don't let them bring their own program discs. Their discs may be infected, and could spread the infection to your system.

7) Don't use copies of programs that illegally had the copy protection removed.

Software publishers are becoming increasingly aware of the potential threat of viruses, and many of them sell packages designed to detect and remove viruses, or minimize damage. Check with your company's IS (Information Services) department or software supplier. If you aren't computer literate, ask for advice from someone who is.

Viruses aren't the only form of computer crime you have to worry about. Criminals with the technical know-how are tapping into systems and stealing services, information, and most certainly money. Here are some tips to make sure your system isn't infiltrated. Make sure your employees are aware of these procedures. If you're an employee, suggest these tips to your boss:

• Don't give your computer password to anybody, not even your best friend as he or she may unwittingly pass the information on to the wrong person. The company should also have a 'secure' record of your password in the event of an emergency.

• Don't tape the password to your computer, or write it in your rolodex. There's only one place to store a password where nobody else can gain access to it: your memory.

- When choosing a password, avoid the obvious. Birth dates and phone numbers are okay for playing the lottery, but they make you an easy mark for would-be criminals.

- Make sure your computer is programmed to reveal unauthorized use or program alterations.

- Separate computer programmer and operator functions.

- Make sure programs contain a statement of ownership.

- Monitor and log all inputs and outputs.

- Use special devices and procedures to control access to the terminals and to certain files.

For more information you can contact:

National Center for Computer Crime Data, 2700 N. Cahuenga Blvd., Suite 2113
Los Angeles, CA 90068
Phone:(213) 874-8233.

Technology and automation are making life easier for everybody. Need cash but the bank is closed? Use an automatic teller machine (ATM). Want to order an item over the phone? Use your credit card. Want to listen to the messages on your answering machine when you're away from home? Use your remote messages retrieval number.

Technology is also making it easier for criminals to gain access to your money, your credit account, and your personal information. Here's how to protect yourself:

- When choosing a personal I.D. number for your bank or other access cards, avoid birth dates, phone numbers, or names. That makes it easier for a criminal to guess your I.D. number.

- Memorize all of your I.D. numbers and keep them to yourself. That way nobody else can use your bank card or listen to the message on your answering machine.

- Don't give your credit card number to anyone who solicits you by phone. In a common scam, solicitors tell you that you've won a prize and ask to verify your credit card number. Once they have the number, they can charge purchases by telephone to your account.

- Carry only essential credit cards that you know you are going to be using. Keep the others at home in a secure place.

- Always rip up your carbons after a credit card transaction, and cut a credit card in half before discarding it or returning it for cancellation.

- Be careful when giving out your social security number. For example, if you are opening a bank account, make sure the other customers waiting in line can't overhear you giving your number. To be safe write pertinent security information down and show it to the bank employee (i.e. social security number, mother's maiden name, place of birth or access password).

Don't give your credit card number to anyone who solicits you by phone. Once they have the number, they can charge purchases by telephone to your account.

- When making a transaction at an ATM, or when dialing your answering machine, make sure that nobody is watching when you input your I.D. number.

- Thieves often lurk near ATM machines at banks. Be alert when you enter and leave the ATM area and try to avoid using an ATM after dark.

- If your credit, bank, or social security cards are lost or stolen, report it immediately.

Do not allow a clerk or anyone to write your credit card and/or ID number on the back of your checks. This procedure is routinely done as a verification of your identity even though it is now illegal. Be courteous in complying with requests to produce one or two pieces of I.D. but be assertive in your request that they do not record your personal, confidential data on the back of the check. To allow the establishment to do so will serve no functional purpose other than to expose you to fraud, forgery, and other rip-offs. And, it doesn't provide the establishment with any additional protection. The credit card company and the state agency that issued your I.D. are not liable (nor would they accept the responsibility) for stolen, lost, forged or insufficient funds checks.

Criminals in possession of such confidential personal information can also obtain a copy of your credit history. One method of retrieving these records is to submit a written request to a major credit bureau with the required service fee (usually under $30). And within a few days the criminal would have a complete computer print-out of your credit files. However, if the crook used a computer to steal

> *Do not allow a clerk or anyone to write your credit card and/or ID number on the back of your checks.*

the information, the process would be complete in a matter of moments. So, protect yourself from this invasion of privacy by insisting that no personal information be written on the back of your check.

Merchants operate under the illusion that unless you possess a credit card, your honesty, integrity, and solvency is questionable. Therefore they squeeze you to prove your good character by producing a credit card. Your plastic gives them the false confidence of prompt payment. This procedure is a form of security for the merchant and/or clerk to view your credentials, without the unnecessary risk of writing the information down.

Your good credit is a valuable and powerful asset and you should safeguard it with prudent diligence. A con artist can and will ruin your good credit standing if given half a chance.

Many crafty methods are used to obtain consumer credit files. I don't pretend to know them all or even most of them. Why? Stealing credit is considered an art by thieves in the business. And, like any other form of art there's infinite variety as well as ego involved.

CREDIT SCAM #1:
The Executive Rental Home/Apartment

This scam involves ostensibly listing an executive house or luxury apartment on the market for rent. The residence may be occupied or vacant. It doesn't really matter which to the credit con artist. He may have access to an occupied home because he has paid the homeowners (usually personal friends) to be allowed to show their home to 'marks' under the pretense that it would be available for occupancy in 45 days. Or the criminal may go through the time and expense of actually renting an executive home to play out the scam. In the case of the latter he would ultimately rent the home to *one* of the home seekers for a small profit. The new tenant would subsequently be permitted to stay by the legitimate owner.

What's he really after? Remember those credit applications everyone filled out in order to assure the owners of the home that they were trustworthy renters? Well, the con man has collected nearly a dozen rental/credit applications. These documents contain crucial credit and bank account information. Now, just imagine what a creative con artist could do with *your* well established credit.

CREDIT SCAM #2:
The Scavenger Hunt

Another insidious technique is for the credit thief to dress in shabby clothing in an attempt to disguise himself as a scavenger. He would then commandeer a supermarket shopping cart and roam the alleys of business districts, rambling through trash dumpsters, collecting aluminum cans and guess what? Discarded credit applications. Hot spots where completed credit applications can be found are in the trash cans and dumpsters of car rental agencies, finance offices, real estate brokers and furniture stores. I'm told by Scavenger Hunt operators, that actual use of this method can net 25 workable applications per week.

Depending on what the crook has in mind, she can obtain phony identification in your name very easily. Getting such I.D. is no problem. Any halfway decent street hustler knows how and where to do this. Mostly, hustlers will only need I.D. if they plan to obtain a cash bank loan or set up a checking account or fictitious business as the catalyst to a bigger scam. In your common run-of-the-mill credit rip-off scam, I.D. is never needed because most of the purchases are made from mail order and major department store catalogs via telephone. Airline, theater, concert and major sporting event tickets, are bought in super-abundance and later sold by scalpers.

Whenever you're asked to fill out an application that requires or requests information of a financially sensitive nature (i.e. bank, credit card account numbers and/or bank balances), be aware that your privacy is being invaded. This information is not necessary for a legitimate business to conduct a credit check. All they need is your name, birth date, social security number, employment, and address. And, in most instances your social security number and date of birth is optional. Unless you're certain and comfortable with the reason and true purpose for requiring this information, tell the requester your views on the issue.

Businesses are the hardest hit by credit fraud. The consumer cannot be held liable for merchandise fraudulently charged to their accounts. They may be charged a small service fee by the credit issuing company (which is usually only $50). Their financial responsibility is limited. However, the merchant's business can be ruined by check forgery and credit fraud.

CREDIT SCAM #3:
Fine Furniture For Less

Bruce C., is a 42-year-old, black convict sentenced to seven years for credit fraud. Bruce operated a unique business in Los Angeles. He trafficked in furniture. Bruce would window shop and browse through fine furniture stores on a regular basis. His intent was not to buy furni-

---

Whenever you're asked to fill out an application that requires or requests information of a financially sensitive nature, be aware that your privacy is being invaded.

ture, but to steal furniture through credit fraud. But before he cheated the store out of the furniture, his first act of business was to locate a buyer.

Bruce's customers were exclusive and referred by previous customers. All his customers knew that he could get them the furniture and/or appliances of their choice for 50 percent off the marked price. Bruce and his customer would go together to a furniture store selected by the customer. If the customer saw an item or complete set of furniture that he wanted, he would alert Bruce to his choice. Bruce insisted only that they select at least $3000 worth of merchandise, and that they pay cash in full upon delivery.

After the salesperson confirmed availability, Bruce's customer would continue to browse or wait in the car, while Bruce arranged for a no-money-down credit purchase. His phony credit application would be approved on the spot, or within three days. Occasionally a small down payment would be required. Bruce always preferred renting a truck and picking up the furniture but every now and then it was more expedient to rent a small apartment for the sole purpose of delivery.

Bruce specialized in obtaining false credit through the use of credit applications he found in trash dumpsters. If the credit applicant was within ten years of Bruce's age, more or less, and male, he would obtain fake I.D. and impersonate the real Mr. So and So. He operated his 50 percent furniture business successfully for fifteen years. He enjoyed a well-to-do lifestyle with two luxury cars, a mobile home, a motorcycle, a 30-foot cabin cruiser and a two-story, four-bedroom, three-bath suburban home. And, of course, he owned a house full of fine furniture.

THE OUTCOME

The law of averages finally caught up with him in 1987 when he applied for $8500 worth of credit in a furniture store as Mr. Paul S. Wingate (not the true name). His problem was that his salesperson turned out to be Vicki Wingate, the wife of Mr. Paul S. Wingate.

CREDIT SCAM #4:
Keep An Eye On Your Time Card

Bruce shared another of his credit gathering methods with me. He told me that most large hospitals', department stores' and supermarkets' time clocks and employee time cards are easily accessible. All you have to do is watch the shift change. When workers are reporting to work, subtle observance will lead you to their time cards. Often, time cards are openly displayed. Bruce says he patiently waits for an opportune time then casually gets to the time cards and copies the names and social security numbers off several cards. Then, without arousing suspicion, he leaves the vicinity.

Bruce then gets fake I.D. cards made in the names of the men and women whose names and social security numbers he'd fraudulently obtained. Bruce knew many women that were willing to use illegally obtained identification to defraud. With any one of his female accomplices he would target the *NO CREDIT NEEDED* exploitation furniture stores throughout Southern California. All that is required to get merchandise from these establishments is a *contrived* paycheck stub, a steady job, identification and 10-20 percent cash down payment. Then presto, instant credit.

Whether or not these legitimate furniture stores are exploitation establishments is irrelevant. For Bruce to use that as justification to defraud these businesses is ridiculous. I was not impressed or fooled by his 'Robin Hood' excuses. Neither was the judge.

The fact is that small businesses are often ruined by con artists such as Bruce. Many of these businesses carry their own contracts, which means they absorb all the risk. And in the cases where financing was available, insurance companies soon discontinued their relationship with stores that were repeatedly victimized.

CREDIT SCAM #5:
Name Badges and License Plates

Another technique Bruce told me about involves memorizing employee names from badges, desk and/or door plaques. What do you think door plaques have to do with credit fraud? Here's how he ran the scam.

Bruce would enter a place of business and purposefully observe the employees that wore name and title badges and/or had their name and titles on their office doors or desks. Two or three names and titles would appeal to his intuition (hustlers are superstitious, sometimes they have an intuitive good or bad feeling about a 'mark' or scheme), in which case he would return at a later date to follow his instincts.

Suppose Bruce had a good omen about a man sitting behind a desk with a slate that read, "Mr. John Q. Public, Manager, or Jane Doe, Receptionist." He would park in the parking lot near the time his 'mark' would be leaving work. When his victim left the building he would get car license number information. (A victim who carpooled was dropped.) With the license number of the car (which was hopefully an expensive or late model), he would pay a small fee to have the department of motor vehicles run a registration check. If the name of the registered owner matched the name on the desk, he would be encouraged. Now, the only remaining obstacle to getting access to his victim's good credit is to establish who owned the car; either the victim, a bank or another lending institution. A lending institution would be best as this would mean the car was bought on credit and payments were still being made.

Now Bruce knows a little more about his 'mark'. First, he knows where John Q. Public works; second, he knows his job title or position; third, he knows where he lives; fourth, he knows one of the 'marks' creditors.   To obtain more personal information Bruce would call the personnel office of his victim's employment, pretend to be the credit manager of a local furniture store, and ask for verification of John Q. Public's employment, his starting date, social security number, birth date, and salary. Most personnel offices of large companies gladly supply this information as a courtesy to their employees.

Bruce next calls the lending institution that financed John Q's automobile. He identifies himself as their customer, Mr. Public, and explains his payment book and financial records were recently lost in a house fire. He doesn't know his account number, he would like them to look it up, and then forward him a duplicate payment book, along with a copy of his original credit application. He explains that his copy of the application was also destroyed and he customarily retains the credit application of all his credit purchases for his records in case he's ever audited. Bruce as Mr. J. Q. Public asks the creditor to forward his request to his 'temporary' address. Until his house or apartment is refurbished he would be staying at 'such and such' address. The address given would be a private mail receiving business Bruce recently rented under his 'marks' name. Occasionally, the lending institution will ask Bruce (Mr. Public) to identify himself by his social security number, birth date, or date he began working at his job. Of course, Bruce already has this information from the employer's personnel office.

Within a week (if all goes well) Bruce has possession of the credit application which contains enough pertinent data to abuse his victim's good credit rating. However, if Bruce had preferred a more expedient route he would consult a major credit bureau and request a copy of 'his' credit files. All the credit bureau would require of him is his name, birth date, social security number, address, place of employment, and a small service charge (usually under $30). With this route Bruce would have a computer printout within the hour. Of course he would have to produce I.D. in the credit holders name and age.

Once the data is received, there's no hurry to work it. Some credit rip-off artists let such information lie dormant for months, others work it immediately. It depends on their volume of customer requests. Whenever they do work their scam the odds of getting away with it is highly in their favor. Credit hustlers are a minority in any men's prison. Most male criminals have no patience for such swindles. Or maybe the prison system has so few of them, not because only a few men are involved, but so few are apprehended.

Small businesses are the ultimate victims. The initial victim (the impersonated consumer) may feel violated, embarrassed, and outraged, but their actual monetary loss is small when compared to the merchant. One of the major reasons, according to the Small Business Administration, that thousands of small businesses go out of business each year in the United States is due to poor management and a plethora of criminal perpetrators. Many life savings are lost, dreams and futures destroyed. And whenever businesses are forced to close, jobs are lost. We have often heard small businesses referred to as the backbone of America. If this is true, then in my opinion, fraud operators, forgers, and other business malefactors are America's osteoporosis.

TIPS AGAINST CRIME

Here are my tips to help reduce your risk of credit card fraud.

- If you want to put additional security on your business and personal checking account, I suggest that you speak with the bank manager regarding implementing *your own* supplemental security system. Here's how it works.

  Pick any ten numbers in sequence from 1 through 100. (For example; 79-88, or 21-30, etc.) Then inform the bank manager that you will write one number in sequential order following your signature on each check. (For example, John Doe 79, on the next check, John Doe 80, John Doe 81 etc.) When you reach your tenth check or John Doe 89, you start over with number 79 again. You must record these code numbers in check records as you normally duplicate any transaction. The bank should be compelled not to honor any of your checks that do not bear your security protection number.

  If a con artist comes into possession of any of your blank checks, even if he's adroit enough to duplicate your signature, and knows all pertinent personal data used as bank security, (i.e. date of birth, social security number, mother's maiden name, etc.) chances are he will not know

---

Implement your own supplemental security system. To do this, speak with your bank manager.

your secret security system, unless the information came from a dishonest bank employee.

- Keep a list of your credit card numbers, expiration dates, and the number of each card issued in a secure place.

- Watch your card after giving it to a clerk. Take your card back promptly after the clerk is finished with it and make sure it's yours.

- Tear up the carbons when you take your credit card receipt. Void or destroy any incorrect receipts.

- Never sign a blank receipt. Draw a line through any blank spaces above the total when you sign receipts.

- Open credit card bills promptly and compare them with your receipts to check for unauthorized charges and billing errors. Report promptly and in writing to the card issuer any questionable charges. Written inquiries should not be included with your payment. Check the billing for the correct address to send any written inquiries. The inquiry must be in writing to guarantee your rights.

- Never give out your credit card number over the telephone unless you have initiated the call.

- Never put your card number on a post card or on the outside of an envelope.

- Sign new cards as soon as they arrive. Cut up expired cards and dispose of them promptly. Cut up and return unwanted cards to the issuer.

- Leave infrequently used cards in a secure place.

- If any of your credit cards are missing or stolen, report the loss as soon as possible to your card issuers. Some companies have 24-hour service and toll free numbers printed on their statements for this purpose. For your own protection, follow-up your phone calls with a letter to each issuer. The letter should contain your card number, the date the card was missing, and the date you called in the loss. If you report the loss before a credit card is used, the issuer cannot hold you responsible for 'any' subsequent unauthorized charges. If a thief uses your card before you report it missing, the most you will owe for unauthorized charges on each card is $50.

For information on improving your business security:

Small Business Administration
Office of Consumer Affairs, 1441 L Street, NW,
Room 503-D
Washington, D.C. 20416.
Phone: (202) 653-6170 or 653-7562
(or consult your local directory)

• • •

Referrals:

Small Business Administration, Books, 1441 L Street NW, Washington, DC 20416. Phone: (202) 653-6365. The following booklets are available: Preventing Retail Theft, Free; Outwitting Bad Check Passers, Free; Preventing Burglary and Robbery Loss, call for cost.

U.S. Department of Commerce, National Bureau of Standards, Law Enforcement Standards Laboratory, Gaithersburg, MD 20899. Phone (301) 921-3161. Standards for doors, windows, and alarm systems. Ask for list of free materials.

N.C. State Crime Prevention Division, Dept. of Crime Control and Public Safety, 512 N. Salisbury Street, Raleigh, NC 27611-7687. Phone: (919) 733-522. Offers booklets. Call for current list.

Insurance Information Institute, 110 William Street, New York, NY 10038. (212) 640-4768. List of target standards for business plus related crime prevention publications.

American Society For Industrial Security, 1655 North Fort Meyer Drive, Suite 1200, Arlington, VA 22209. Phone: (703) 522-5809. General security information for members plus a monthly magazine, and other relevant publications.

National Burglar and Fire Alarm Association. 1133 15th. Street NW, Suite 1000, Washington, DC 20095. Phone:(202) 296-9595. Distributes a brochure entitled "Security Alarm Services For the Small Business.

National Retail Merchant Association (NRMA), 467 Sixth Avenue, New York, NY 10001. Phone:(212) 244-8780. They offer many booklets and audiovisuals on retail crime prevention. Call for current publications list.

International Association of Credit Card Investigators, 1620 Grant Avenue, Novato, CA 94947. Phone: (415) 897-8800. Clearing-house on credit card crimes.

Mitre Corporation, 7525 Colshire Drive, Records and Resources Dept., McLean, VA 22101. Phone (703) 883-6001. Ask for a free copy of Security and the Small Business Retailer.

American Planning Association, 1313 East 60th Street, Chicago, Il 60637. Attention: BookStore. Phone (312) 955-9100. Provides, for $14.95, a basic, yet comprehensive citizen planning guide called, "The Citizen Guide To Planning."

Federal Crime Insurance Program, P.O. Box 41033, Washington, DC 20014. Phone: 1-800-638-8780. This program provides reasonably priced crime insurance for companies and individuals within eligible jurisdictions. For more information call or write the above address. There are additional organizations that are helpful in providing information or materials concerning crimes against business. Contact the Resource Center at NCPC for more information.

Legal Aid and Legal Services offices help individuals who cannot afford to hire private lawyers. There are more than 1,000 of these offices around the country, staffed by lawyers, paralegals, and law students. All offer free legal services to those who qualify.

Funding is provided by a variety of sources, including federal, state and local governments and private donations. Many law schools nationwide conduct clinics where law students assist practicing lawyers with these cases as part of their training.

These offices generally offer legal assistance with problems such as landlord-tenant relations, credit, utilities, family issues (such as divorce and adoption), social security, welfare, unemployment, and workmen's compensation. Each Legal Aid office has its own board of directors which determines the priorities of the office and the kind of cases handled. If the Legal Aid office in your area does not handle your type of case, it should be able to refer you to other local, state, or national organizations that can provide advice or help.

Consumer Credit Counseling Services, (CCCS):
Counseling services provide assistance to individuals having difficulty budgeting their monthly expenses. Many organizations, including credit unions, family service centers and religious organizations offer some type of free or low cost credit counseling.

The CCCS is a non-profit organization that offers money management techniques, debt payment plans and educational programs. Counselors take into consideration the needs of clients, as well as the needs of the creditor when working out a debt repayment plan. You can find the CCCS office nearest you by contacting the National Foundation for Consumer Credit, Inc., 8701 Georgia Avenue, Suite 507, Silver Spring, MD 29910. Phone: (301) 589-5600.

Chapter 6

Confidence Games and Other Such Scams

There are some crimes against which the major defense is foreknowledge. These crimes against the consumer are called confidence games. How do they work? A con-man gains your confidence, usually takes your money or personal property and leaves before you realize you've been scammed. Confidence scams are limited only by the imagination of the criminal and the gullibility of the victim. Here are a few of the more popular and successful confidence games. Read on and then next time, when a con-man comes calling, you won't be the victim but the victor.

CONFIDENCE SCAM #1:
The Perfect Rental Home

Here's how this scam works. A couple goes to a rental agency and contracts for their assistance in locating suitable housing. The agency charges a nominal fee for this service. A list of available homes for rent is given to the clients, and from that list they select a couple of homes to view. (Or the couple may discover houses for rent in the classified ads of the local newspapers.)

The couple telephones for an appointment to view the home on a preliminary inspection. Upon their visual approval of the residence, they are required to complete a credit application, plus pay a small non-refundable deposit to show sincere interest (earnest money). Due to minor improvements, the landlord or agent informs the clients that they won't be able to move in for three weeks. Then this landlord opens a briefcase inside of which are rental agreements, a rent receipt book, and credit applications. He pulls out the credit applications and may hand you a business card as well.

The routine pitch continues with the landlord mentioning that a credit and reference check will be done and that the balance of the first month's rent is due upon application acceptance. A few days later the deal is consummated, and as the new beguiled tenants anxiously await their move-in day, the swindler continues re-renting the same property.

TIPS AGAINST CRIME

- Be suspicious if the agent's direct line connects to an answering service. Dialing a number that's intercepted is more likely legitimate than dialing an answering service direct.

- Be suspicious when there's no "For Rent"signs on the property. (Renter frauds never put 'For Rent' signs out, for worry that the legitimate owners or a suspicious neighbor will foil their scam.)

- Whenever meeting a landlord/agent for the first time at the property site, and *before* you hand over your money, ask for identification and/or write down the license plate number of his vehicle.

- While waiting for the application approval, call the utility companies and order future service. Inquire at the utility company if there have been any other recent inquiries of new service. If so, this is a danger sign! If not, call again a few days later with the same concerns.

Be suspicious when there's no "For Rent" signs on the property.

- If you suspect fraud, have another party call the answering service number to inquire as to the availability of the same property. If this landlord/agent returns his call and makes an appointment to show him the vacant house, consider yourself fortunate. You've just saved yourself a lot of money and misery.

- Notify your local police or sheriff's department, and local newspaper and ask them to investigate.

CONFIDENCE SCAM #2:
Phony Property Loans

Eric S., a 49 year-old con man serving six years for embezzlement revealed to me a scam he has used for years in obtaining fraudulent real estate loans. The scam has two victims: the lending institution and the homeowner. As in the home renting scam, rental property is involved. The con artist scouts for a well kept attractive house for rent. When one is located, the con artist puts a deposit on the property to express sincere interest and promises to return with the balance in a day or two, or as mutually agreed upon. During this brief period, Eric says, he would ascertain the name of the legal property owner through the tax assessor's office. If the property was owned by a corporation, he would move-on to another prospect.

Once Eric obtained possession of a suitable rental property he would arrange to get false ID, in the name of the owner. After the ID was received, the con artist would open a bank account under his new name. Then he would obtain a credit report from at least two major credit bureaus on

---

If you suspect fraud, notify your local police or sheriff's department, and local newspaper and ask them to investigate.

the credit status of the legitimate property owner. Eric evaluated the extent of the owner's indebtedness and checked for liens and judgments against the property. A certified copy of the deed could be easily obtained.

After ascertaining the equity in the property, Eric S. would contact a few finance companies and have a representative come out to *his* home to give a home appraisal, and discuss the possibilities of a home loan.

With the lending institution that qualified him for the largest loan (usually over $75,000), he would officially apply for a loan, using the true owner's identity, credit history and property deed as credentials.

According to Eric and other cons that have played this scam, execution of the entire operation takes less than a couple of weeks. After a period of time, the check finally arrives and the con artist moves on to another rental property.

TIPS AGAINST CRIME

• Do thorough background checks on all prospective tenants, even the ones you especially like. This includes, but is not limited to; credit, employment, and previous resident checks. Insist on and verify personal references (at least two), and ask to see vehicle registration.

• Property owners should arrange with all major credit reporting agencies to be notified by mail of any inquiries into their accounts. (Send for Sandcastle Publishing's Fair Credit Instruction Manual $20.95 at P.O. Box 3070-TAC, South Pasadena, CA 91031 for the scoop on how to do this.)

- Whenever renting property, get the names, addresses, and phone numbers of at least two family service professionals with whom they have done business for any stable period of time (i.e.: dentist, lawyer, accountant, doctor, stock broker, banker, etc.)

- If there are children of school age in the family, get their names and the school of attendance.

This type of checking may annoy you and take more time than you think it's worth, but it will annoy and deter the potential rip-off artist even more. Legitimate applicants that are in search of a place to live will not be discouraged by your efforts of self-protection.

CONFIDENCE SCAM #3:
You Win the Prize!

Prizes are gifts or products companies make available to consumers as an incentive to order other products. While such a technique is used legitimately by hundreds of companies nationwide, telefraud operators may also use premiums as a *hook* to lure consumers into buying hundreds of dollars worth of merchandise, often at inflated prices.

In a typical example, consumers receive a postcard or a letter notifying them of their eligibility to receive one of several prizes or premiums. Consumers may confuse the offer with a sweepstakes notice. While the prizes or premiums may vary, they often include such luxury items as mink coats, diamond watches, luxurious automobiles, or savings bonds.

> *Property owners should arrange with all major credit reporting agencies to be notified by mail of any inquiries into their accounts.*

After responding to the mailing through an 800 number, consumers quickly learn they have to purchase products or services before they receive the premium. This format is favored by telefraud operators who market vitamins, water purifiers, office supply products, and travel services.

Consumers should be aware of the problems associated with such offers. Even if they purchase the product, the chances of winning the "grand prize" are slim to none. Furthermore, the cost of products or services offered are often inflated. Complaints of non-delivery and poor quality can be expected.

CONFIDENCE SCAM #4:
Business To Business Fraud

Telefraud operators have cleverly capitalized on the business market by invoicing companies for products they never ordered or that are clearly inferior. This fraud relies on the internal accounting procedures of some businesses that may allow invoices for unordered products to be paid.

In this type of fraud, the caller simply inquires about the make and model of a piece of office equipment, and further claims to be conducting a survey or serial number check. In some cases, the salesperson will obtain the name of an office manager or receptionist to whom to send the products without authorization. Statements such as "price increases are imminent, so you must purchase now," or "a death in the family has forced them to liquidate all assets immediately," should alert consumers that they may not be dealing with a reputable company.

"Toner poners" or "paper pirates" are masters at implying that they have done business with a company before.

They often gain valuable information by calling to confirm an order "previously placed by someone else" at the company. Another approach used is aggressive collection tactics to intimidate small businesses into paying for unordered merchandise.

Businesses can defend themselves by verifying the telephone number and address of the caller to check out any business affiliation.

CONFIDENCE SCAM #5:
Credit Repair

Legitimate non-profit financial counseling services are available to help people resolve their own credit problems. Such services charge little or no money for their advice.

Fraudulent credit repair companies however, promise unequivocally to improve or fix a person's credit history, get him out of debt or to obtain credit cards for him - usually for a substantial fee.

As with other types of telefraud, the initial contact for credit repair fraud does not have to be over the telephone. Many times, the fraudulent companies favor classified advertising in newspapers.

The ads are characterized by promises to erase bad credit, remove bankruptcy and liens from personal credit files, to end all debt, or to obtain credit cards, regardless of credit history. Generally, the ads feature such headlines as "Bad Credit, No Problem," and an 800 number as the contact. In my opinion, if obtaining credit cards "regardless of bad credit history" was such a guarantee, at least one credit card company would start such a program.

CONFIDENCE SCAM #6:
Employment Ads

There are job seekers that are lured by newspaper ads of employment opportunities to fraudulent school recruiting offices. The recruiting offices advertise unskilled jobs available (i.e. warehouse workers, truck drivers, nurses aids, file clerks, receptionists, etc.). When the job seeker calls the number, they're assured that dozens of jobs are available through the many companies their office represents. The caller is then given an appointment to come in for an interview.

Once at the interview for the non-existent job, the applicant may be told that the company offering the listed positions will only consider applicants with technical experience in a specific field, or because they work with government contracts, they must hire 'X' amount of students this year. The interviewer would strongly imply that the applicant was not sufficiently qualified to secure stable employment with good pay without first learning a marketable trade. They would promise to find the applicant a full or part-time job only on the condition he enroll in one of the trade schools which the fraudulent employment service represents.

The vocational schools would, in turn, inveigle the applicant to apply for a government student loan for their training. They work hard to insure the applicant that the government will not only loan him money to secure a trade but will also supply him with a cost of living income while attending school. These desperate citizens would then eagerly borrow thousands of dollars from the government for their education.

The school then pays an average of ten percent of the total tuition to the recruiting agency and the student receives a few dollars monthly for necessary expenses.

Reimbursement would be included in loan payments to the government. The student unfortunately, receives inferior training and may eventually default on his government student loan. This fraud continues throughout the U.S., mainly among the minority communities.

TIPS AGAINST CRIME

Job seekers should be alert to fraudulent job ads. These ads share a few characteristics:

- Repetitious advertisements
- The same phone number in several locations of a classified ad circular referring to different blue collar, low paying or unskilled jobs.
- Unnamed companies offering several immediate openings.
- Very little information about the job or company can be obtained on the phone.

When calling these numbers you should ask the following:

- Is this the actual company for which I would be working in the event that I'm hired?
- Are there any loans to be applied for or contracts to sign?
- Are you a training referral agency?

Any of these questions will save you time and money, if firmly asked and honestly answered.

If you feel their answers or the ad is deceptive, complain to the newspaper in which it appeared. Also report the company to the Better Business Bureau nearest you.

If you wish to obtain job training in another trade, contact your state employment office and public school system and inquire about low cost or free job training programs.

CONFIDENCE SCAM #7:
Business Ventures

Deceptive employment offers prey on our basic need for financial success. These ads are often characterized as the classic work-at-home opportunities, or the once-in-a-lifetime offer to participate in a distributorship program or multi-level marketing opportunity.

As with telefraud, the consumer's first contact with the fraudulent business or employment promoters often comes through print and broadcast advertising, particularly classified ads in newspapers.

The deceptive ads for business ventures promise unrealistically high profits in a short amount of time while requiring little or no investment. The ads generally feature graphics that depict consumers holding a fistful of dollars, or surrounded by luxury items. Oftentimes, the ads claim to be "giving away a secret plan for success", or "no experience is needed" to make "big, fast, profits."

Ads for overseas employment opportunities generally promise immediate employment in the profession of choice. Advertised salaries are often well above current market rates. Employment fees are generally required before consumers are placed in a job assignment.

CONFIDENCE SCAM #8:
Cellular Telephone Lottery

The Federal Communication Commission (FCC) is now in the process of conducting a public lottery to award licenses for the construction of cellular telephone cells in rural area (RSA's) across the nation. The FCC award program has attracted the attention of a drove of telephone con artists.

Boiler-room salesmen offer to submit the necessary paperwork for entry to the FCC lottery for between $2,000 and $5,000, and promise an almost 100% chance of winning a license. Investors also are provided with grossly inflated estimates of the value of the cellular telephone licenses, which may be resold. Though some of the highly populated RSA's are undoubtedly extremely valuable, others (rural Wyoming and North Dakota, for example) are less certain to be the guaranteed cash cows of which telephone salesmen speak.

The Federal Trade Commission and Minnesota Department of Commerce have taken enforcement action in recent months against promoters of cellular lottery scams. One estimate has it that the boiler-room activities of cellular lottery application mills may result, over the next two years, in investor losses of more than $250 million in filing fees alone.

CONFIDENCE SCAM #9:
Telefraud

The most popular fraud-by-phone game by far is the one that pitches investment. Be especially alert for such fraud. I want to emphasize the necessity for precaution in this area.

You may be called out of the blue, or as a follow-up to investment literature you've received (but probably never requested).

The investments you're most likely to be offered are precious metals, such as gold and silver, oil and gas lease lotteries, rare coins, mining venture, and penny stocks. You're urged to sign up right away, because they claim you have to catch the investment's "big move".

Once you've agreed to buy an investment, the con artist rarely buys it, but will usually ask you to pay for the bogus investment by getting a certified check from your bank and having it ready to give to an overnight mail carrier who is sent to your home. A week or so later you may even receive a confirmation letter stating that the investment has been made.

Most consumers don't realize they have been victimized until they call and find that the company's phone number is disconnected or they are no longer contacted about "hot" investments. Some victims have invested hundreds of dollars. Others have lost their life savings.

Mike D., a 36 year old accountant serving 5 years for telemarketing and wire fraud, described to me a typical victim rip-off scenario by his fraudulent boiler-room operation.

One day while watching a TV commercial that claimed there was a lot of money to be made in gold and silver investments (many TV viewers trust everything they hear and see advertised on the tube) Donna H., decided to call the "800" number shown on the screen. When she called, the man she spoke to seemed trustworthy and caring. In subsequent calls, other friendly salesmen convinced her to invest in soybeans, wheat, cotton, and even the cellular telephone lottery. Donna kept buying these investments for nearly six months, until her son found out and advised her to stop.

Unfortunately, Donna had already lost $23,000 her life savings. During that six months she had raised the money by cashing in virtually sound investments, such as savings bonds and CD's.

"Why were we so successful? I would call Donna up a few times a week, just to see how she was doing and stroke her emotionally. These conversations were interspersed with calls and brochures outlining the latest good invest-ment. I would sometimes tell Donna how much I enjoyed talking with her and how she reminded me of my first grade teacher that I loved so much. She actually looked forward to my calls."

CONFIDENCE SCAM #10:
The Water Filter Scam

Mike B., revealed other telefraud scams during our talks. This one plays on our desire for good health.

"Consumers would receive a card from Mothers' Health Products Inc., of Denver, informing them that they were *Absolutely Guaranteed* to win either a brand new cus-tomized fully equipped Dodge van, a $10,000 cashier's check, a diamond watch or a $3,000 U.S. savings bond. These advertisements would always be sent out of state to decrease the chance of an irate consumer storming into the offices of the private mail service center hired to receive our replies."

"When the long distance calls came pouring in through the 800 number supplied, our sales pitch would be typical of the following: The salesperson would identify him/her-self using a false name (assigned by the company) and inform the caller, *To qualify for a prize, you'll have to order a $418 purifier. I'm sure you're aware of the shocking dete-rioration of your drinking water.* The salesman would add something like, *We're drinking processed sewer water!* We claimed that Mother's Health Products' purifier removed rust, dirt, algae, chlorine, bad taste, odors, pesticides, her-bicides and man-made petrochemicals. *It's the only unit that totally purifies and the only one that can legally be sold in Great Britain,* (a lie.)"

The $418 sale is made via major credit card. In about two weeks the countertop purifier would arrive. On the casing would be the words: "This product .... is designed to remove objectionable tastes, odors and color from municipally treated tap water." There would be no mention of rust, dirt, algae, chlorine, petrochemicals or anything else.

The facts are that retail stores sell water treatment equipment with replaceable filters for about $40 that the manufacturers say remove chlorine and 90% of lead and copper. A system said to take out 99.9 percent of bacteria and 98 percent of pesticides was advertised in the Washington D.C. area recently for $110.80. Water can be almost completely purified by distilling; Sears sells a brand name home distiller for around $200.

The prize? Of course, they would win the diamond watch. The price tag would show $750., but they actually bought them at local department stores for $60 to $80 each.

CONFIDENCE SCAM #11:
The Anti-Drug Effort

"In this telefraud" Mike went on to tell me, "we would solicit funds to fight the war on drugs and offer prizes to our financial contributors. A postcard would be sent to known charity supporters obtained from a mailing list. They would be 'guaranteed' prizes. All they had to do to support our organization was to purchase a fabulous package costing just $459. They would then become eligible for their prize of camp equipment or an all expenses paid trip to Las Vegas. The package, which could be a tax deductible donation if given to a church, school, youth group or drug program, consisted of an educational videotape, 250 bumper stickers, a magazine and a plaque."

When the caller purchased this anti-drug package via major credit card, Mike's office forwarded him a camping outfit which included a plastic 12' x 10' tent, two wool blankets, a camping booklet and three outdoor cooking utensils, valuing $85.

The War Against Telefraud

A few prize promoters are in trouble with state and federal authorities in California. Eric B., drew a five year prison term in 1988 for his part in a scheme in which victims were told they had won one of five grand prizes; including a car or a Caribbean cruise. To receive them they had to put out $962. for "premiums" to avoid gift taxes. None of the promised prizes were ever delivered to the victims.

In Nashville, Tennessee, the U.S. District Court issued a temporary restraining order against a fraudulent company, which had sent an estimated 470,000 certified letters telling people in 48 states they had won one of five prizes, including $10,000 and a Ford Taurus. Callers were informed they had to pay a $26.50 "handling" charge to qualify for it but didn't learn until later that their award was a Florida vacation that could cost them well over $1,000 and was subject to numerous restrictions. Postal officials accused the company of operating an illegal lottery because people had to pay to win. They may get their money back if the court order is made permanent according to a report from the Council of Better Business Bureaus.

According to the New York Times, New York state has charged two Manhattan companies with false advertising. The companies mailed millions of sweepstakes notices that led consumers to believe they had won valuable jewelry. It wasn't valuable. New York's Attorney General, Robert Abrams, said his office had pieces of the prize jewelry analyzed and discovered that some of the diamonds were too small to be seen with the naked eye.

In Tulsa, Oklahoma, a 'boiler-room operation' had civil charges filed against them by the Attorney General who accused the operators of misrepresenting their shower water treatment units. The operators claimed that their unit could remove a variety of impurities from tap water. Actually, the units may be dangerous because the filters are sealed inside the casing, they can't be removed or replaced, and after awhile may release contaminants that have built up over time.

In Texas, a married couple, formerly of Great Falls, Virginia, face trial on mail fraud charges alleging that they sent 26 million letters promising BMWs, cash or other major prizes to people who visited condominiums in several vacation resorts. Instead, "winners" received a book about the 1984 Olympics, a 1982 Car Racing book, a set of knives or redemption certificates that would require the person to pay to get an item. The couple was freed on $50,000 bond following their indictment, and departed from Texas.

A few months later, California authorities arrested the pair on a similar charge. They were living in Rancho Santa Fe, a millionaires' playground in Southern California. They had changed their name and drove a new Silver Rolls Royce, lived in a five bedroom Spanish-style house that rented for $5,000 a month, and ran their exclusive direct mail business out of an exclusive pink adobe office complex. Both are currently serving time in California prisons, and will be extradited to Texas to stand trial after their commitment is met in California. The man wishes to remain anonymous and is serving time with me here at Soledad State Prison.

Walter E., operated a fraudulent mail marketing company that told about 6,000 people that as part of a marketing survey they had been selected to receive a three-person Electrasport boat with outboard motor. All they had to do was pay $138 for shipping. They got an inflatable vessel with a plastic motor resembling a "glorified egg beater" that cost about $42, including the shipping charge. Walter E., accepted a plea bargain offer and pleaded guilty of mail fraud.

Tips Against Crime

The General Rule:

> If it sounds too good to be true, it probably is. You don't have to be naive or stupid to fall for a con—just a little too anxious to take advantage of a great offer, a little too reluctant to look cheap, a little too hopeful of a miracle cure-all, or simply unaware. Your best defense against fraud and con games is to be informed. And, most importantly, if you do fall victim to fraud, report it to the police. It may be embarrassing, but it's the only way con-artists can be stopped.

Don't Get Hooked By These Classics

CONFIDENCE SCAMS #12-17

12) A couple of strangers tell you they've found a large sum of money or other valuables. They say they'll split their good fortune with you if everyone involved will put up some *good faith money*. You turn over your cash, and you never see your money or the strangers again. You've been a victim of the "Pigeon Drop".

13) A so-called bank official asks for your help to catch a dishonest teller. You are to withdraw money from your account and turn it over to him so he can check the serial numbers, or do an audit. You've been a victim of the "Bank Examiner" fraud. No legitimate official would ever ask you to withdraw your money.

14)   Someone offers you a painless way to make money. You invest so much cash and you solicit others to do the same, and they solicit others, and so on. Just like a chain letter. This is the classic "Pyramid Scheme" also known by other names (i.e.: airplane, skyscraper, or cherry tree). Sometimes the initial investors are paid a small dividend, but when the pyramid crashes—as it always does—everyone loses. Except the few people at the top who have just skimmed the money and never invested any.

15)   A newspaper ad promises a great income for performing unskilled tasks at home (such as stuffing envelopes). Work at home schemes always emphasize easy work, convenience, and high hourly pay. Sound too good to be true? They are. After you've paid for supplies, or a how-to book to get you started, you find there is no market for the service or product you're supposed to produce at home. And there is no way to get your money back.

16)   Shortly after the death of a relative, someone delivers to your door a leather-bound bible that your deceased relative allegedly ordered. Or you get a bill in the mail for an expensive item on which you must make the remaining payment. This is a "Funeral Chaser" who uses the obituary notices to prey on bereaved families. Don't be conned. You are not responsible for anyone else's purchases, and if the claim is legitimate, it will be settled by the estate.

17)   The cause sounds worthy and the solicitor is sincere, but it's a charity you've never heard of, or has a confusing name. Before you give, ask for identification on both the charity and the solicitor. Find out the charity's purposes, how funds are used, and if contributions are tax deductible. If you're not satisfied with the answers and feel something is not quite right, don't give.

CONFIDENCE SCAM #18:
Bargain Repairs

A fire inspection turns up the need for repairs that will cost thousands of dollars. A contractor offers you a special half-price chance to have your house re-roofed because he has a surplus of material from another project. Don't be conned. These are favorite tricks of dishonest firms or individuals who prey on consumers and especially home owners.

Always get several estimates for any major work. Don't be pressed into accepting a one-day only offer. Never pay for work in advance. Withhold full payment until the work is completed, and pay with a check or money order, not cash. Always get references for a contractor and check their record with the Better Business Bureau and county licensing agencies. Get a written contract (and make sure you fully understand it) before the work is performed.

CONFIDENCE SCAM #19:
Everlasting Health

- Miracle Drug Melts Away Cellulite.
- Restore Hair the Safe and Natural Way.
- Vitamin Treatment Prevents Cancer.

These scams take advantage of the natural desire to be attractive and to prevent or cure disease. The cures or treatments may be harmful, and they can be fatal if they prevent you from getting sound medical treatment. Be wary of exaggerated claims or secret ingredients. Before purchasing any of these cure-alls, check with your doctor.

If it sounds too good to be true, it probably is.

CONFIDENCE SCAM #20:
Free Vacations

Someone calls and wants to verify your VISA card number because you have won a free gift. Hang up! Do the same if an executive travel club calls and says you've won a free vacation if your credit card is current. Don't give them any details about your credit cards. Someone who has your number can make charge purchases by phone to your account.

What If It Happens To You?

Very few frauds are reported to law enforcement authorities. Victims often say they are too embarrassed to admit they were duped, and believe the police can't do anything, or think fraud isn't a police matter.

You're wrong. The police are very interested.

Did you know you can cancel a charge? Under the Fair Credit Billing Act you can contest a charge within 60 days of being billed, on grounds that the product was misrepresented.

Write to the institution that issued the card, state that there was a billing error and why you think there was a mistake. Enclose copies of any documents that support your case. By law, the institution must investigate and cancel the charge if it finds in your favor. You do not have to pay the charge or any interest while it's being contested.

If you feel you've been ripped-off you may complain to:

1) Federal Trade Commission, Telemarketing Fraud, Room 200, Washington DC, 20581.

2) The Better Business Bureau. Check your telephone directory for the Bureau nearest you, or write to the Council of Better Business Bureaus, 4200 Wilson Blvd., Arlington, VA 22203.

3) Postal Inspection Service. Write to the Postmaster of your local post office, attention: Postal Inspection Service/Fraud Branch.

4) National Consumers League, Alliance Against: Fraud, 815 15th Street NW, 516, Washington, DC 20005.

5) Write a letter to the editor of the local newspaper to warn others.

What else can you do?

1) Start a program to educate community residents about common frauds and remedies available for victims.

2) Lobby your city or state legislators to establish a hotline that people can call to check contractor's or solicitor's credentials.

3) Call your consumer protection agency (listed in your local telephone directory) police department, or district attorney, if you think you've been the victim of fraud. Many cities now have special economic crime or consumer fraud units to help victims, and stop the con artist from hurting others.

4) Alert your co-workers, neighbors, and neighborhood watch group to any known con games in the area.

5) Always use common sense. Bear in mind that if a seller has to promise lavish prizes to bring in business, whatever is being sold may be over-priced, low in quality or not much in demand.

CONFIDENCE SCAM #21:
Lost and Found Pets

Many items are lost in major cities each day. The unfortunate owners of these lost, misplaced, forgotten, or stolen items are often very upset. They offer large cash rewards for the safe return of their belongings.

In some incidents criminals were responsible for the disappearance of the valuables and are also responsible for their safe return, as they play a double role in their scam, thief by night/Good Samaritan by day.

Here's how this scam is run: A thief steals a pet and waits for the reward notice to go up. He telephones the number in the notice and claims to have 'found' the lost animal and arranges to return it. The original owner is so elated that he gladly pays the thief a handsome reward.

These types of scams are quite common. Just take a glance at the 'lost and found' column of any big city newspaper and count the number of potential scams at work. Very few (if any) of these missing valuables have been reported to the police. And many of the notices include the announcement, "Reward: no questions asked."

"I played that game for years," says Oscar T., a 39-year-old inmate, serving nine years for his third burglary conviction, "until I figured out better ways of working the con." Oscar told me, "with this method you don't have to ever steal anything and there's practically zero percent chance of getting busted." The game requires two partners and an animal. The 'mark' or 'victim' is not the owner of the animal (as you may think), but the 'Good Samaritan' trying in good faith to return the 'supposedly' lost family pet. Here's how it's played. Watch out for this one. It's tricky.

Everyday in the local newspapers throughout many communities in Los Angeles County there are hundreds of free dogs and cats offered to anyone willing to provide a loving home. What Oscar's partner, Saul, and he did on a regular basis was to pick-up these animals, mostly puppies and small dogs, and keep them well fed and groomed until they were needed.

For this to be successful, both con men had to be bilingual. Saul and Oscar are fluent in both Spanish and English.

When they were planning the geographic location for their operation only cities and communities that were predominately Hispanic were targeted. They would scout for locations in those communities where checks are cashed (i.e. banks, check cashing outlets and supermarkets). The plan would be to approach customers exiting these locations and get them to hand over $150 to $300 in exchange for the lost dog and an opportunity to collect a $1000 - $2000 reward. Their monetary goal was to rip-off at least six people each day they worked.

They then decided on the community and located at least six outlets where checks were being cashed. Then off to an isolated or semi-isolated telephone booth where they would tape up the coin deposit slots and place and 'out-of-order sign on it. And copy the phone number.

"Now we rush back to Saul's house, where the animals are kept and select six of them to use. We have previously purchased dozens of expensive looking dog collars, blank name tags, and an electric engraving pen.

We engrave a name for the animal on one side of the name tag and the phone number of the public phone on the other side with the added word 'Reward'. We would then write in a memo pad the name we'd given each animal and any distinguishing marks and color, and size of each animal."

Oscar smiled and told me they were lucky because he owned a van, which made hauling around six dogs easy. "Now we headed for the phone booth to set up our post and make sure our 'out-of-order' sign was still on the phone." Oscar said that Saul would be driving his own car. One of them would stay near the public phone, with the van and waiting dogs. The other would take 'one' dog in the car and drive to one of the previously staked-out check cashing outlets. They alternated assignments each working day.

(In this example, Saul is at the phone booth and Oscar is working the prospects.) When Oscar gets to the vicinity of his first destination he telephones Saul to alert him that he's about to begin work. Now Oscar lingers near the business establishment stalking his prey with the animal in his arms or on a leash.

When a potential good prospect is spotted (which is any adult well-dressed Spanish person), Oscar (shabbily dressed but always clean), asks the person in his native Spanish language, "Pardon me, sir, do you speak English?" If the gentleman answers, (in the Spanish language), that he does speak English, Oscar knows immediately he has a fish on a hook, and with skill and perfect timing he can reel him in. (This entire conversation is conducted in Spanish.) Oscar asks him to please do him a favor. He explains to the gentleman that he found the animal this morning in the park as he was jogging. "The dog has been following me all day. I checked his name tag and called the telephone number, so I could tell the master of the dog that I have found his lost pet. But, when I called the number on the name tag, I found that I couldn't communicate by message because the man on the phone speaks only English." (The psychology behind this tactic, Oscar explained to me was that most bilingual Hispanics are eager to flaunt their skill in front of those who aren't).

If the *mark* agrees to lend his assistance, Oscar removes the name tag and hands it to the man. And together they walk to the nearest phone booth which is usually just a few yards away. As they walk towards the phone, Oscar is continually thanking him and saying how he would have hated for the animal to just roam loose, for the streets are full of dangers. But unless he could deliver the dog within the hour he would have to reluctantly turn the animal loose because he had a dentist's appointment at 1:00 PM across town and the dog wouldn't be allowed to board the city bus. By now, the *mark* is in the phone booth speaking English to Saul on the other end of the line.

"Hello, my name is Mr. Lopez" (for example) "have you lost your dog?", asks the Good Samaritan.

Saul excitedly replies, "Have you found Rocky? Oh my God! This is great! Tell me, please, is the dog you found a mixed breed about one foot high, with dark brown fur and a white right paw?"

Mr. Lopez would turn to inspect the dog and assure Saul that it is, indeed, 'Rocky'. Saul might add something like is he wearing a red dog collar or does his right ear stand straight up and his left ear bends half-way down? Mr. Lopez would exclaim, "Yes, yes, that's him all right."

"Please bring him to me", says Saul, "my little girl has been crying herself sick for two full days that 'Rocky' has been missing. It's all my fault", Saul declares, "I carelessly left the back gate ajar when I put out the trash and Rocky wandered off. There's a $1,500 cash reward if you can deliver him to me after 6:00 o'clock this evening. Can you do that, please, Mr. Lopez?" asks Saul, "I must be leaving home now to pick up my employer at the airport, says Saul, I'll definitely be home by six."

"Yes, of course, I'll bring him to you," says Lopez, (assuming Oscar does not understand English) "you did say $1,500, right?" Now Lopez anxiously writes down the (false) address given to him by Saul. (When he gets off the phone the conversation returns to the Spanish language.) Oscar now asks about the words 'Rocky' and 'Reward' engraved on the name tag and asks what those words mean, "I'll receive money?" Before Lopez can respond, Oscar continues, "Let's go there now to receive the money, it may be as much as $350, maybe $400. Come on, Mr. Lopez, please drive me there so I can receive maybe $400, I'll split it fifty-fifty with you."

"Sorry, Oscar," says Mr. Lopez "but the master of the dog won't be home till much later. I'll take the dog for you and contact you later if there's a reward." (Greed has entered into the mind of Mr. Lopez and now he's plotting to rip-off Oscar.)

Oscar vehemently disagrees, claiming that he doesn't have a phone and doesn't have transportation to be hauling this dog all over town. Oscar tells Mr. Lopez that there will certainly be a big reward for such a well groomed dog with an expensive collar. He then suggests that Mr. Lopez give him half of what was sure to be a $400 reward. He (Oscar) says that once before he'd found a dog and returned him and the owner paid him $400. Mr. Lopez then says, "are you sure I'll get at least $400?" Oscar assures him that the dog he found before wasn't even as good looking a dog as 'Rocky' and he was paid that sum. And, two years ago, Oscar tells Mr. Lopez, that his wife returned a lost cat to the owner and received $500.

All the while, Mr. Lopez, is thinking about his $1,500 profit for returning this pet in a few hours. As expected, he eventually pays Oscar the $200, or he might even swindle his way down to $150.

Oscar receives the cash and hands over the worthless animal to Mr. Lopez. They shake hands and depart company, each man laughing inwardly and feeling proud of himself for the con game he ran on the other.

Oscar now drives back to their post. After sharing a laugh with his accomplice, he retrieves another animal and heads for their second location. Oscar repeats this scheme until all six dogs are in the hands of six greedy (otherwise) Good Samaritans.

TIPS AGAINST CRIME

- The only sure way to prevent this or something similar from happening to you is to never be too anxious to make a few quick, easy dollars.

CONFIDENCE SCAM #22:
The Ol' Diamond Switch-a-roo

Peter M., a 45 year-old inmate sentenced to 13 years for armed robbery, has worked several years in Las Vegas casinos as a dealer, pit-boss, and part-time magician.

In prison he often wins money in card games and through mind quizzes and card tricks. As a dealer, in card games, he had the ability to know what cards each man at

---

Never be too anxious to make a few quick, easy dollars.

the table held, even if he dealt the cards with his eyes closed. He also possessed acute dexterity. Nobody ever accused him of cheating when he broke them in card games. In prison, unless you can prove your accusations, you don't accuse anyone of anything.

Peter had a reputation for lifting the wallets from prison guards and replacing them minutes later. During his brief possession of their billfolds he would copy their credit card numbers and expiration date. Then he would give this information to various associates on the outside via coded telephone messages. They, in turn, would order thousands of dollars worth of merchandise, by phone, using these names and credit card numbers. The goods would be sent to private address mail service centers and later sold. Peter's associates would then forward him 10 percent of the money and deposit forty percent into his outside personal savings account.

One day Peter confided in me and showed me some recent bank statements he had received from the bank. The bank records revealed that during Peter's three years of continuous incarceration he had saved over $93,000. By his own calculations he estimated that by the time he is released from prison (within four more years), his personal outside savings would surpass two hundred thousand dollars, not to mention perhaps up to twenty thousand in his inmate trust account.

During the many private conversations about our past, we joked about the various swindles, scams, and con-games we had perpetrated. It was during one of his trips down memory lane that I learned of the, "ol' diamond switch-a-roo."

It seems that when Peter was a college student in Chicago, during the mid-60's, he concocted a scheme to earn extra money through the carelessness of pawn shop brokers. He had noticed that when a pawn shop customer pawned a piece of jewelry, after a brief 'loop' inspection the broker placed the jewelry in an envelope and wrote the date, customer's name, the amount borrowed, and a concise description of the item on the outside of the small package. Peter says he decided to browse through many pawn shops to assure himself of their standard policy and procedure in accepting jewelry as collateral for a loan. After getting their routine down pat, he proceeded to the next phase of his scheme.

Peter went to a jewelry store and asked for a booklet of all the jewelry available for purchase. The jeweler obliged with a free booklet with colorful pictures, prices and stock numbers for their merchandise.

The entire life savings of Peter M. was approximately $850. He withdrew all but $25. There were several rings in his $800 price range. He took the booklet with him to the costume jewelry department of a major department store. The jewelry there ranged from $5 to approximately $35. With the naked eye these pieces appeared to be a good quality product. Their general appearance and weight was identical to many of the rings and watches he had physically examined at the jewelry store.

Peter purchased a $10 ring that was identical to an $800 ring he had examined and tried on in the sumptuous jewelry store. Then he rushed back to the jewelry store and purchased the $800 ring that was identical to his $10 ring. He was very concerned that when the clerk wrote him the receipt for this major cash purchase that every detail of the receipt was correct (i.e.: his name, address, date, description of purchase, and the amount paid).

After careful contemplation, he took the ring to a pawn shop two weeks later. The expensive ring was worn on the index finger of his right hand and the cheap one was subtly obscured in the palm of his left hand. Peter browsed aimlessly through the pawn shop purposely appearing reluctant to state his business, a nervousness Peter was sure any experienced pawn broker would covetously recognize. The pawn broker finally asked if he could be of any service. Peter unresponsively began to explain that a close relative had recently passed away and he needed $100 for train fare to attend the funeral. As he spoke, Peter had his hand clenched at chest level and with his left thumb he conspicuously stroked the ring. The proprietor beckoned with a backward throw of his head for Peter to follow. As Peter slowly inched forward, looking sentimentally at his ring, he would mumble that his grandfather was the best man in the world, and that he wouldn't want to miss this opportunity to pay his final respects.

In the all too familiar stoic demeanor of pawn brokers, Peter heard him snap, "Let me see that there ring, boy?" Peter slowly removed the ring from his finger and humbly gave it to the heavyset store owner. The man looked at the ring with his naked eye and expounded, "You can't get no more than $20 for this." Peter stood silently as the broker grew impatient for his reply. Then he broke the silence with, "Just a minute, boy, let me take a closer look." He withdrew a small eyepiece that resembled a miniature microscope and re-examined the ring. After scrutinizing the ring under the eyepiece for 15 to 20 seconds he announced "Forty dollars is the best I can do."

Peter put up mild resistance but gave in to the more experienced man's offer. He watched carefully and listened inattentively as the broker spoke of how sorry he was about Peter's grandfather and that he truly wished he could do more. As the broker spoke, he also perfunctorily did what Peter expected him to do. When he had completed filling out the envelope, he dropped the ring inside and was just about to lick the glue on the flap, when Peter exclaimed, "Wait, I've changed my mind."

The broker grumbled something under his breath and handed Peter back the ring. Peter accepted the ring with his right hand and in a continuous flow exchanged it to his left hand, and in plain view of the broker, slipped the cheap fake on his right index finger. Then Peter placed his right hand flat down on the counter and asked the moneylender if he could make it fifty dollars. The man said, "all right, all right, fifty dollars it is, but not a cent more. It's only because of your grandfather that I'm doing this." The broker watched as Peter removed the 'fake' from his finger and handed it to him. The broker immediately dropped it in the envelope and sealed it. He wrote the new amount of fifty dollars on the envelope and stapled a ticket to the outside of the envelope. He tore the stub of the ticket off and gave it to Peter. Then he went to his cash register and rang up 'no sale' and withdrew two twenties and one ten dollar bill and pushed the money at Peter.

As Peter walked toward the door he looked back over his shoulder and shouted, "I'll be back in three or four days for my ring."

The proprietor replied, in a sarcastic voice, "Sure you will."

Though Peter was forty dollars to the good and still in possession of the genuine diamond ring, this fraud doesn't dwindle and die there. To merely walk out of a dozen 'hock' shops about town with a few crumbs from a fat man's table, was not Peter's idea of a scam, but only the bait. And in his debut, the bait had been gobbled.

This would be a battle of wits. Pawn brokers had earned a notorious reputation in Chicago during the 60's, for being crafty, shady operators. The newspapers frequently published articles warning the public to be wary of pawn shop brokers. It had become common knowledge that some pawn brokers would cheat their customers. One trick, in particular, that they were quick to perpetrate, was to accept genuine jewelry as collateral on small loans and switch the diamonds in the jewelry with frugal facsimiles. The pawn shops had been pulling this switch for years. Three shop owners were under a grand jury indictment on fraud charges and they were proclaiming their entire profession dibbled and dabbled in a shady deal now and then. Although this was during the winter season, the climate for these businessmen was hotter than July.

Three days passed, and Peter returned to the pawn shop to reclaim his 'valuable' ring. When he entered the establishment the jingle bell above the door alerted the big man behind the counter of his presence. The proprietor gave Peter a glance of acknowledgment, then re-directed his attention to his elderly female customer that was purchasing a used four-slice toaster at a price higher than the new ones featured in a downtown department store. It was Peter's assumption that the old woman, probably didn't read the newspapers regularly (if at all) or she would have to seen the advertisements by the major department stores promoting four-slice toasters for 50 percent off. Nor did she travel about town often, or she would have known that there was a community thrift shop about six blocks away where used items could be bought at a 'true' value. Nevertheless, he held his peace.

As the previous customer quietly shut the door behind her, the pawn broker was shutting the door of his register, after ringing the sale price of $12.95. "What can I do for you this morning", inquired the store owner.

"I'm here to pick up my ring," replied Peter, "that I pawned the other day."

"Oh, yeah, yeah, I remember" said the pawn broker, "got your ticket?"

"Sure do, sir," said Peter, "right here." Peter extended his ticket stub forward and watched it impolitely snatched from his hands. As the broker walked away to his file cabinet to produce the merchandise, Peter stood relaxed and patient, waiting for his ring, with fifty-four dollars in his hand.

The owner returned to the counter with the envelope and dumped the contents out into his own hand. Then laid the ring on the counter and Peter, simultaneously, did the same thing with the cash. As the shop owner picked up the money to count the small denominations, Peter picked up the 'fake' diamond ring. Right after Peter picked up his ring, he said in an assertive tone, "What the hell is this?"

"What the hell do you think it is?" the shocked broker snapped back.

Peter, holding the ring closer to his eye, inspected it, then denied that the ring was his. He accused the man of operating a clip-joint and demanded to be given the valued ring he had entrusted with the establishment.

The broker demanded to see the ring again himself. As he scrutinized it with his 'loop', (microscope), and other examining instruments, Peter produced his original $800. purchase receipt and demanded satisfaction. The broker was visibly shaken by this time, admitting that he can't explain what had happened. He defended his integrity but Peter didn't budge.

"I don't know what's the matter either," said Peter, "All I know is that I brought you a ring worth $800, and now you try to foist this fifty cent piece off on me. I'm not leaving here until you give me 'my' ring or accept your responsibility and pay me its value."

The broker desperately wanted to palliate this imbroglio before other customers arrived or the police and/or newspapers were informed. Peter of course, didn't let up and the broker was in no position to be stubborn. He knew that the benefit-of-the-doubt was with his customer. He began an attempt to compromise the situation. He reasoned that all jewelry had a one to two hundred percent mark-up price. And although Peter paid $800 for the ring, the true value is between $200 and $400. He suggested that they split the difference and offered an instant cash settlement of $300 which included the fifty dollars originally given as a loan. Peter pretended to contemplate this offer and then apprehensively gave in. The broker quickly counted off $250 from a lower desk drawer and returned the $54 Peter had given him. Peter signed a receipt for the money as reimbursement for lost property.

Peter left the shop wearing the 'fake' ring and $300 richer. That scam played for four months, covering twelve pawn shops. Each paying between $150 to $400 to settle a quick claim. Peter boasted that when he retired that scam he had made over $3000, and still had possession of both rings.

"Over twenty years passed," says Peter, "before I ever considered working the Ol' Diamond Switch-a-roo again. Then in 1985, my girlfriend desperately needed $25,000. Her request to me for a personal loan was gently denied. However, I promised to help her raise the money by her five day deadline. I taught her the trick of my college days. She was a diligent student. We purchased twenty-five pieces of costume jewelry, all ladies rings, at the cost of $800. Then I drove her from one expensive department store after another, throughout the County of Los Angeles. In the jewelry department she would browse for rings that were identical to the 'fakes' resting in the trunk of my Rolls Royce."

"Her assignment was to only show interest in rings priced over $5,000, that were close enough to one of our 'fakes' that an inattentive clerk wouldn't notice the switch." She would be very well groomed and conservatively dressed in quality clothing. He says that until she returned and informed him that she had seen a look-a-like, Peter would stay in the car. Then she would carry the fake look-a-like with her back into the store. To assist her in some way, he would arrive at the jewelry counter a few minutes after her. They would pretend not to know each other and when she had the genuine diamond in her hand, he would distract the clerk with a question.

Peter's protégé would ask to see the expensive ring and switch it with the fake. This was all done before the clerk's eyes. Peter said that his friend had gotten so good that after the fifth switch he stayed in the car.

Within four days she had switched twenty-five fake pieces for valuable rings. Peter bought all the jewelry from his friend for $25,000 and later sold it to a 'fence' for a $15,000 profit.

TIPS AGAINST CRIME

Peter said he was surprised that jewelry stores didn't exercise more precaution in their handling of jewelry. All salespersons handling genuine diamonds should be trained to use a 'loop' (an eyepiece used to scrutinize jewelry). And they should examine each piece before passing it to a customer and re-examine it when the customer passes it back (even if it was two seconds later).

All jewelry customers should insist that jewelry is appraised before they pay a large sum for it.

All jewelry customers should insist that jewelry is appraised before they pay a large sum for it. You may be paying thousands of dollars in a reputable jewelry store but unbeknownst to the store, or you, that item might be a worthless facsimile. You should also have it independently appraised immediately after you buy it.

CONFIDENCE SCAM #23:
Fortune Telling Frauds

Superstition is firmly imbedded in the hearts and minds of millions of Americans. And the number of new converts is forever increasing. These people are vulnerable to one of the oldest, cruelest and easiest to perpetrate frauds known to any crook I've ever met. Spiritual Advisors, Card Readers, Palmists, Fortune Tellers, Witch Doctors, Voodoo, or any other mystic know-it-all should be avoided like the plague. Especially when it involves the personal health or finances of you or your family.

There are more criminals selling 'hope' than there are selling 'dope', and in these days and times, that is difficult to imagine. The 'dope dealers' and the 'hope dealers' customers have a few very noticeable traits in common. They disproportionally lack higher education, are haunted by fears, feel oppressed, their lives seem unmanageable, they have low self-esteem or unrealistic superior self-images and they're generally without a sense of true serenity.

Many con artists have switched their specialty to living off the fears and unhappiness of others.

Victor S., a 52-year-old man sentenced to 7 years on conspiracy and fraud charges, said he bilked superstitious clients out of fortunes in his Mystic Advisor scam.

Victor says he adorned himself in full length robes beaded with glitter, ornaments, and gold. He was never seen without a turban and ropes of gold around his neck and several expensive rings on each finger.

He also published a 'How-To' book on spiritual advising which he advertised in the supermarket tabloids and sold for $9.95. Victor says thousands of his book customers set up their own spiritual advising, palm reading, psychic healing, or fortune telling shops after reading his book and taking his ten week, $395 home study course.

Victor went by the alluring title of "Prophet Ptolemy" when he resided in Texas, "King Tarquin" when he lived in Florida, "Swami Isthmus" in Ohio, and "Pharaoh Osmanli" in California. He encouraged his many students nationwide to use catch titles also.

"Our major income is supplied by people with financial and love problems. Those are the two categories that are the root of our business. Other targeted groups are those with judicial concerns (criminal or civil), those concerned about their health, or safety or the health and safety of a loved one, those that want to speak to their dearly departed, and those wanting general good fortune in their lives. Our enterprises sell candles, incense, prayer cloths, sacred rocks, sacrificial vials of blood (animal and human), good luck powders, herbs, dust, perfumes, chips of wood and blessed beads."

"If our client happens to be a person with substantial financial means, our goal would be to convince him he is not being cured because an evil spell is upon his money. He would be discouraged from giving the money away to charities, relatives, or friends. For, if he passed along anathematized wealth, it would surely bring pernicious times and diminish God's light upon them. After all, look at the evil it had brought to him. Bit by bit we would gnaw away his wealth by coercing him, through brainwashing tactics, to 'destroy' large sums of money."

"In practically all the money destroying incidents a ritual of prayer and chants is held. The evil money is wrapped in paper and thrown into fire or a deep body of water (supposedly). The money, at one point, leaves the possession of our client/victim and, at that moment, a switch is made with an identically wrapped bundle of torn newspapers. It is this bundle that gets the ax."

"If our client happens to be of meager, or low income, then wealth is what we would promise. They would be brainwashed into believing that our 'worthless products' (candles, incense, etc.) were the key to their imminent good fortune. These people are nickel and dimed for years. Because life will forever manifest many ups and downs. They're slowly conditioned to being devoted to the misconception that all of their good fortune is due to their faithful compliance. And all their misfortune can be remedied by more vehement prayer, a greater show of faith, more donations and costly services."

"The business is booming. Once you get a person to pay you a second time for goods, services, or consultation, chances are you'll see them again and again. It's like a drug addiction and the only true cure is their ability to manage their own affairs without a crutch."

The following advertisements were taken from the classified ad columns of several newspapers throughout the United States.

Mother Dixon
Your prayers will be answered by the gifted religious healer who hears my prayers. Love and marriage problems? Are you sick, unhappy, unlucky, or disgusted with life? Does bad luck seem to follow you everywhere you go? Do you have Stomach aches, Headaches, Weight, Rheumatism, Back, Nature, or Sleeping Problems? Is someone dear to you drinking or drifting away from you? FREE LUCKY CHARM WITH READING.

Sister Houston

I guarantee success where all other readers fail. There is no heart so sad or home so dreary that I can't bring Sunshine into Life such as: Luck to the poor, Reunite the Separated, Help the sick and ailing overcome their enemies. Restore lost nature. One (1) visit will convince you I'm the one to help. Satisfaction guaranteed.

DR. DIRTY

I GIVE ADVICE ON EVERYTHING. Dr. Dirty will answer one (1) question by phone. My dirty work can help you when everything else has failed. It could be that one of your main problems is that you haven't used anything dirty, you've been trying to be good and kind, sometimes using a little dirty work will go a long way in this world. Dirty work is not for everyone, if you think there's something wrong in using dirty work, please don't call, but if you want things to be better for you and don't care what you use to make it better, then call. I guarantee my dirty work will stop the problems you are having with marriage, sweetheart, boyfriend, fiancé, evil cross conditions, unhealthy bodies, get rid of evil pains, restore lost nature, protection from witchcraft, hoo-doo, voo-doo, and black magic. With my dirty work I will stop your suffering the same hour you see me and talk to me. Quit trying to be so nice, end your suffering today, use dirty work and have a good life. Using dirty work will never fail. It'll stop you from having so much hell, it'll stop spells, curses, bad luck and jinxes. All my dirty work is done in private, confidential, secret consultations. Call and talk. For Appointment and Directions On Where to Come and see Dr. Dirty call 24 hours a day 7 days a week.

Mrs. Kennedy - Spiritual Reader

Are you facing difficult problems? Do you have a drug or drinking problem? Has the one you love left you and you want him back? Are you feeling ill and want to feel good again? If so, see Mrs. Kennedy today, she guarantees to help you with all problems. Over 25 years experience in spiritual guidance.

Rope of Hope

Prayers answered and wishes won. Century old PROVEN theory. History and affirmation with ROPE OF HOPE and Crystal.

Christian Healer

Sister White. The lady with Miracle Powers. Results in 1 hour. Happiness, Success, and Peace of Mind with problems in Marriage, Health, Business, Love, Loss of Nature or Job. Specializes in removing all Evil Spells and bad Luck through Her God Gifted Powers. I solemnly swear to help you where others have failed. I bear a reputation for my Honesty and Integrity. Sister White reunites loved ones back together. If Doctors don't know what is wrong, if it seems like you have no where to turn. One visit will convince you she has the power to help. Call for Free Miracle Prayer.

Appendix A
Clean Up Your Neighborhood

Crime prevention begins at home. But it shouldn't stay there. In fact, neighbors working together can make one of the best crime-fighting teams around. Whether you live in a small town or a big city, it's easy to get involved in crime prevention. There are a lot of things you can do: reporting crime, working with kids, learning about our justice system. It's up to you.

Report crime! Sounds easy, doesn't it? But only about half of all crimes are ever reported. Too bad, because police can't do anything if they don't know what happened. They say information from people like you is the key to solving many crimes. Even an anonymous tip is better than no report at all. So, next time you see something suspicious, don't hesitate. Call the police as fast as you can.

Law enforcement experts say that the battle against crime is well on its way to being won when people take a few simple precautions. Keeping doors and windows locked and making sure keys don't fall into the wrong hands are some examples. It's surprising, but burglars don't always force their way in. Almost half of the time, they enter through an unlocked door or window, or they use your "extra" key. The fact is, victims lose more than $400 million a year from these "no force" burglaries! That's a high price to pay for a crime that could be so easily prevented.

It's surprising, but burglars don't always force their way in. Almost half of the time, they enter through an unlocked door or window, or they use your "extra" key.

Here's another important fact. Half of all home burglaries occur during the day when alert neighbors could
spot the thieves and call the police. In hundreds of communities, concerned citizens are doing just that. They're part
of a Neighborhood Watch, Block Watch, or Citizen
Crime Watch. The names may differ, but the idea is the
same: neighbors looking out for each other. Check with
police or the sheriff department to see if your community
has such a program. If so, join up. If not, start one! It's
easy. Get together with neighbors on your block and surrounding streets. Start by sharing crime prevention tips.
Then exchange home and work telephone numbers and
information about daily routines, planned vacations or visitors, scheduled repairs or deliveries. That way, your neighbors know what to look out for. If neighbors spot an unfamiliar car in your driveway or activity in your home while
you're away, they know they should call the police.

Here are a few other ways for individuals to help rid
their neighborhoods of crime:

1) **Become a silent observer.** These are ordinary
   citizens—seniors, shut-ins, house caretakers and
   others who are in the home daily—trained by the
   police to observe their neighborhoods and report
   any suspicious events. Such a program has been
   very successful in Battle Creek, Michigan where
   silent observers have been reporting crimes
   since 1970.

2) **Organize or join a citizen neighborhood
   patrol.** Again, these are ordinary citizens who
   live in neighborhoods where street crime is a
   problem and most residents are afraid to venture
   out, especially at night. These patrols equip
   themselves with noisemakers and two-way
   radios. They walk their neighborhoods in the
   evenings, blowing whistles when they see some-

thing suspicious and reporting information to the police. If individuals within the patrol have CB radios in their cars, they can organize a radio patrol with police assistance. The New York City Police Department reports that 13,000 volunteers have enrolled in its civilian motor patrol. And police officials claim that more than 300 arrests were made in just one year thanks to reports by these concerned citizens.

3) **Organize or join a tenant patrol.** Many apartment dwellers have formed such neighbor teams to help prevent crime in their buildings. Tenants take turns screening visitors and patrolling halls. They use walkie-talkies to communicate with each other and with a security guard or police. They also meet occasionally to discuss security and learn more about crime prevention. Many tenant patrols also offer escort services for residents who fear going out alone.

Whether or not you join an organized group, you and your neighbors can make crime prevention part of your daily routines, just by watching out for each other. Remember though, it's your job is to *report* suspicious activities to police. Its *their* job to handle the suspects.

What Are You Watching Out For?

• Someone selling watches, radios, TVs or other valuables "dirt cheap" out of a motor vehicle.

• A stranger hanging around the playground befriending the children.

> *It's your job is to report suspicious activities to police. Its their job to handle the suspects.*

- Your neighbors are on vacation, but there's a window open on the first floor.

- A stranger in the neighborhood knocks on front doors, then walks around to the back.

- There's an abandoned car in an alley.

- Someone is running down your street with a stuffed pillowcase, a suitcase, a TV, or a valuable item.

- You are awakened late at night by a loud scream, glass breaking and/or dogs barking.

Sometimes the signs of a crime are obvious, sometimes they're not. Trust your eyes, your ears, and your common sense. Anything unusual may point to a crime.

What Facts You Should Note

- What happened?

- Was anyone injured?

- What did the suspect look like? Describe suspects as carefully as you can, noting unusual features such as scars or tattoos.

- Was a car involved? Were there any passengers in the car? Also, describe the car, noting color and make and any unusual features. If possible, get the license plate number.

- Everything you can possibly recall. Remember, no detail is too trivial!

Reduce Your Neighborhood's Risk of Victimization

Now that you and your neighbors are looking out for each other, take a look around. Does your neighborhood have large, poorly lit public park areas, streets and sidewalks crowded with cars and people from outside the neighborhood, unattended vacant lots and wooded areas? If you answered "yes" to any of these questions, then there are countless opportunities for crime in your neighborhood. Crooks can come and go, unnoticed. They just disappear into the crowd.

Maybe your neighborhood is different. Are streets and sidewalks used mostly by local people? Do children play in the parks and playgrounds? Are there public recreation areas where local residents often get together? If you answered "yes", count yourself lucky. This kind of neighborhood typifies a new approach to crime prevention that seeks to create a "small town" environment within large cities.

Appendix B

Youth Development Programs

1 **The Challengers Boys and Girls Club**
5029 S. Vermont Ave.
Los Angeles, CA 90037
Phone: (213) 971-6161

L.E. Dantzler, a former school custodian, founded the Challengers in 1968. In 20 years, the program has evolved from a fledgling effort operated out of Dantzler's pickup truck into a network that caters to 25,000 participants (90 percent of them Black) and juggles a budget of half a million dollars.

The club works to prevent juvenile delinquency and promote development of children from 6 to 17. Club members are exposed to athletics, arts and crafts, photography and cultural activities. They are also given tutoring and homework assistance, guidance counseling, may join rap sessions and learn leadership skills. Parents are an important component in the program's success.

2 **The Fifth Ward Enrichment Program**
4014 Market St., Suite 105
Houston, TX 77020
Phone: (713) 229-8353

Founded in 1984, this program is situated in the Fifth Ward of Houston, where the population is 97 percent Black. The program targets boys 11 to 14 and operates in two elementary and two middle (junior high) schools.

Most of the program's participants come from single-parent, female-headed households and are considered *at risk* of becoming criminals, teenage fathers or school drop-outs. They are singled out by teachers and counselors because of *counterproductive behavior.* Participants meet before or after school or on weekends. The program's academic component focuses on writing and vocabulary skills, history and business topics and current events, including ethical issues in everyday life and training in public speaking. Psychologists and psycho-social therapists provide counseling and help the youngsters with conflict resolution, self-awareness, interpersonal relations, health and nutrition, and sexuality and sexual responsibility.

3   **The Hawk Federation of Manhood Training and Development Programs**
The Institute for the Advanced Study of Black Family Life and Culture, Inc.
P.O. Box 24739, Oakland, CA 94623
Phone: (415) 836-3245

Hawk stands for High Achievement, Wisdom, and Knowledge and that's what Hawk is all about. Its founders, Dr. Wade W. Nobles and Dr. Lawford L. Goddard say that their program tries "to intentionally and overtly influence the values and moral character of young males by reclaiming African traditions of human virtue and mastery." It is a mentoring program which includes an initiation/rite-of-passage ceremony, based on an African model designed to move trainees into the next development stage and help them explore their future responsibilities.

4   **House of Umoia Boystown**
1410 N. Frazier St.
Philadelphia, PA 19131
Phone: (215) 473-5893

In 1968, Falaka Fattah and her husband invited 15 of their son's fellow gang members to live in their home. The idea, says Fattah, was to teach the boys about the strong African family and reinforce that family value system. At present, there are 23 houses. House of Umoja (which means unity in Swahili) and Fattah has hosted 2,000 boys from 73 different Philadelphia gangs.

5 National Urban League Adolescent Male
Responsibility Program
National Urban League, 500 E. 62nd St.
New York, NY 10021
Phone: (215) 473-5893

The Urban League operates a variety of projects in more than 25 cities. In Detroit, for example, the program focuses on group and individual counseling, Black heritage, personal health, sexuality and fatherhood. The Urban League of San Francisco runs a mentoring group, in which young boys are matched with African-American male role models.

The League's national office also offers assistance to existing groups and guidance to individuals who wish to put together programs for African-American adolescents. The organization has also sponsored conferences of groups and individuals engaged in efforts to resolve the current crisis of the African-American adolescent male and offers a listing of helpful programs. (Write to the Urban League at the address above for more information.)

6 Rites of Passage, African-American Images
9204 Commercial Ave., Suite 308
Chicago, IL 60617
Phone: (312) 375-9682

Rites of Passage programs operate in 17-plus cities, including Los Angeles, Chicago, St. Louis, Kansas City, Detroit, Dayton, Houston, Baltimore, New York, Newark (New Jersey), and Cleveland. Author and sociologist Dr. Jawanza Kunjufu, one of the program coordinators, believes that the programs combat what he calls the conspiracy to destroy black boys. The two-year program teaches adolescents that they must earn the honor of being called men. Participants study Black history, spirituality, citizenship, community involvement, career development and economics. The coordinators also encourage hands-on activities such as community clean up campaigns.

Appendix C
Compensation for Crime Victims

Victim compensation programs are still relatively new. Programs to assist crime victims and witnesses have been established in almost all states since 1984. In general, the programs:

- Provide financial assistance to victims and witnesses.

- Protect the rights of victims and witnesses.

- Compliment existing efforts to aid special categories of victims, such as rape victims and victims of family abuse.

Victim/witness services may also be provided by non-criminal justice agencies (for example, state or local departments of health or human resources). Many private organizations have also developed programs such as rape crisis centers to assist victims and witnesses.

Most state victim compensation programs help to recover medical costs and lost earnings. Forty-four states, the District of Columbia, and the Virgin Islands provide compensation for medical bills and lost wages for victims. In general, awards may be made to persons injured as a direct result of the crime.

If the victim dies, payment to cover burial and related expenses are generally available to dependent survivors.

Most state victim compensation programs help to recover medical costs and lost earnings.

In many cases, injured *good samaritans* (persons injured while trying to prevent a crime or apprehend an offender) are also eligible for payment.

Most states establish upper limits on payments and do not provide compensation for property losses. In general, payment can be made whether or not the offender has been apprehended or convicted, but most states require that the crime be reported to proper authorities.

State Compensation programs are funded with State administered funds. The 1984 Federal Victims of Crime Act also provides for Federal grants to assist states that have established victim compensation programs.

Restitution programs may pay victims for other losses, such as property damage. Many states also permit victims to recover crime-related losses (including property damages) where a court requires restitution by the offender as a condition of sentencing. Unlike compensation, however, such payments are only available if the offender is convicted and financially solvent.

Many states restrict offenders from profiting from their crimes. Several states require that profits earned by an offender in publicizing details of a crime be put into an escrow account and, if the offender is convicted, used to cover crime-related costs incurred by the victim (including, in some cases, legal fees). Funds not needed to cover victim expenses may be returned to the offender or transferred to a general victim compensation fund. The 1984 Federal Victims of Crime Act also requires that profits earned by Federal offenders be forfeited and used to support Federal grants to assist states with victim compensation and assistance programs.

In general, payment can be made whether or not the offender has been apprehended or convicted, but most states require that the crime be reported to proper authorities.

Legislation strengthens the rights of victims and witnesses. Victims and witnesses may not be intimidated. State laws and the 1984 Federal Victim and Witness Protection Act protect crime victims and witnesses against physical and verbal intimidation where such intimidation is designed to discourage reporting of crimes and participation in criminal trials. Laws generally protect all subpoenaed witnesses but may also protect persons whom the offender "believes" will be called to testify or who may have knowledge of the crime. Some laws also permit courts to forbid defendants from communicating with or coming near victims and witnesses.

Victims must be notified of case progress. A large number of states require that:

• Victims be notified at key decision points in the trial and sentencing of the offender.

• Victims be notified upon release or escape of an offender.

• Victims and witnesses be advised of scheduling changes and of available funds to cover court appearances, victim compensation, etc.

Victims may participate in sentencing, parole, or other custody decisions. "Victim Impact Statements," which describe the financial and emotional impact of the crime on the victim (and may also include victim comments on proposed sentences) are now required in many Federal and State cases to be submitted to the court at time of sentencing, parole, or other custody decisions. Victim impact statements are generally included as part of the pre-sentence investigation report.

A comprehensive Victims' Bill of Rights is included in some state laws. Comprehensive Victims' Bill of Rights laws:

- Protect victims against intimidation.
- Ensure that victims receive notice and are allowed to participate in various stages in the case against the accused offender.
- Such laws may also:
  —Ensure the victims rights to continued employment.
  —Provide medical or social support services.
  —Require the appointment of an "ombudsman" to protect the rights of the victim during the trial period.